Michigan's Town and Country Inns

Second Edition

Susan Newhof Pyle and Stephen J. Pyle

The University of Michigan Press

Ann Arbor

Library of Congress Cataloging-in-Publication Data

Pyle, Susan Newhof, 1952–
  Michigan's town & country inns.

  Includes index.
   1. Hotels, taverns, etc.—Michigan—Directories.
2. Bed and breakfast accommodations—Michigan—
Directories.   I. Pyle, Stephen J., 1950–   II. Title.
III. Title: Michigan's town and country inns.
TX907.P95   1987   647′.9477401   86-30877
ISBN 0-472-08074-1 (pbk.)

To Richard and James Pyle
and Nancy and Michael Ullman,
with our love

Contents

Introduction   1

The Inns   5

Superior
Upper Peninsula and Mackinac Island   9

Land of Little Bays
Northern Lower Peninsula   31

The Southern Shore
Southwestern Lower Peninsula   91

Heartland
Central Lower Peninsula   139

Metro
Southeastern Lower Peninsula and the Thumb   187

Bed-and-Breakfast Reservation Services   223

Index   229

Introduction

There was a time in this state when roadhouses and small hotels were scattered all along the major routes between cities. They ranged from steamy taverns with primitive sleeping quarters upstairs or "around the back" to elegant inns with fine food and furnishings. Many of the lodgings went out of business and were abandoned when freeways came along, routing travelers around small towns and off the back roads. Some were converted to restaurants or office buildings, some caught fire. Some just quietly crumbled until they were finally torn down.

A few of the grand old places have survived the decades of transition and are well known because of their prominent roles in history and their undisputed charm. But with a growing interest in preserving our historic architecture and a yearning in travelers for lodging that is personalized, warm, and memorable, more than 125 inns and bed-and-breakfast homes have opened or reopened throughout Michigan in less than half a decade.

With this second edition, we take you on another adventure across Michigan's two peninsulas and into more than 75 such accommodations. Some are like tiny museums full of turn-of-the-century treasures. Some are rugged and rustic and will intoxicate you with the smell of wood and fresh air and breakfast cooking. They are as different from each other as the individuals who run them. Their differences are, in part, what makes them so endearing. After years of whirlwind weekend research and more than one hundred interviews, we find they still do not blur.

We have tried to portray each place accurately and do not expect that you will like all of them—indeed, if you did, it might mean they were losing the distinctiveness that makes some of them so fiercely appealing. We have been asked occasionally during the past year if we would develop a rating system to guide you in your selection process. That takes us back to a discussion on trying to categorize lodging establishments that have little in common. And it does not begin to address your personal taste, expectations, and previous experiences. We feel that a rating system for this book is not practical and not desirable at this time, but to help you choose the accommodations that will best suit you, please consider the following information before you make reservations.

• First, a little about innkeepers because they are the heart and soul of most inns. It is often in their living room that you will spend the evening chatting with other guests and in their kitchen or dining room that you will continue the conversations over morning coffee. An innkeeper gives a place its flavor and sets the mood, and for that reason you will find an emphasis placed on them in many of the descriptions. We want you to know a little about them so you will have a better feel for the places you visit.

Some innkeepers, you will find, are accomplished artists, athletes, or scholars. A few have had distinguished military careers. Some are quiet and pensive, others are flamboyant. Generally, the smaller the inn, the greater the presence of the innkeeper. Almost without exception, we discovered that innkeepers take great pride in being able to sense which guests would like to be alone and which are up for group discussions on the front porch that may go on until dawn.

Each time we interviewed an innkeeper, we asked what they liked best about innkeeping, hoping for some deeply insightful answers that would make clever quotes. The responses were almost always the same.

"It's the people."
"Don't you get tired of sharing your living room with strangers?"
"Five minutes after they arrive, they're no longer strangers."

Innkeepers have also told us that many of their guests make their own beds, send thank-you letters, bring gifts on subsequent visits, and have become warm friends. Guests have said they visited an inn the first time because of the furnishings and location; they returned because of the innkeepers.

• Many inns and bed-and-breakfast homes do not feature a private bathroom with each sleeping room. If shared or down-the-hall bathrooms do not appeal to you, ask the innkeeper about rest room arrangements. For example, will it make a difference to you if you share a bathroom with one other room? with two? with six?

• The beds at inns vary greatly. Some offer only twin beds; others feature king- or queen-sized, or custom-made antique treasures. Remember that most turn-of-the-century people were shorter than we are today—and so were their beds. If it matters to you, ask about bed sizes.

• Some people can fall asleep on anything. Some require firm, lumpless mattresses. If you fall into the latter category, ask if the mattresses are new or original equipment.

• If it applies, inquire about the inn's policy regarding smoking, children, and pets. Many innkeepers discourage at least two out of three. And while we are on the subject . . .

• Many innkeepers have dogs and/or cats. In almost all cases, we found the pets obedient and their owners quite willing to keep them tucked out of sight at a guest's request. With animals in a house, however, there is occasionally an odor that the owners do not seem to notice, and that visitors—particularly non-pet-owners—can detect the moment they walk in the door. If you are bothered by the presence of a pet, take the innkeeper aside and mention it. They may not be aware of the offense. If you have allergies, phobias, or pet peeves, ask the innkeepers if they keep pets in the house and, further, if the animals are ever allowed into quarters that are shared by guests.

• Some inns have lockless sleeping room doors. Will that bother you? If you are traveling with valuables, ask if the inn has a safe where you may store them.

• Ask what will be included in your room rate: meals, linens, cleaning service, taxi or shuttle service, afternoon tea, admission to local points of interest, access to recreation areas and equipment (tennis courts, bicycles, sailboats, skis, etc.), tips, parking? In this book we have primarily provided information on food or meals included in the price of the room.

• Some of the older inns have built new additions onto the original structure or have constructed separate accommodations elsewhere on the grounds. If you have a preference as to wing, section, floor, or building, let the innkeeper know before you make the reservation and emphasize no substitutions.

• Many inns have a wide range of room prices because of the variety in rooms. If you are quoted a room rate that is more than what you want to spend, ask if a less expensive room is available. If the time of your visit is not important, consider traveling in the off-season. A great many of the inns discount rates substantially after fall colors and before Memorial Day. Many also have special business rates, discounts for extended stays, and discounts for groups renting all the rooms. Rates are listed in this book to give you an idea of the range of prices available. Most are peak-season prices. They are updated as close to press time as possible but may be slightly different from those quoted to you at the time you make reservations. They are subject to change without notice.

• Many inns and bed and breakfast homes are not set up to process credit card payments. If you plan to pay for your room with anything other than cash, when you make a reservation, ask for the house policy on payment methods.

• And now, a word about making reservations. Do. Always. Remember that many of the places described here are private homes. They do not have all-night desk clerks. They want to know when you are coming, and they do not want to find you unannounced on their doorstep at 11:00 P.M. With advance notice, you will find innkeepers to be some of the most hospitable people you will ever meet.

We have spent at least a few hours at each lodging covered here, and in many cases we stayed overnight. During the past five years of researching, many innkeepers have extended to us house courtesies, which have been accepted when logistically possible. We are grateful to the innkeepers for their gracious hospitality. They enabled us to log the several thousand miles of travel it took to compile this firsthand information.

In every case, they have opened all doors to our inspection and have been candid about the offerings and limitations of their accommodations. Nobody likes to see a guest unhappy with a misrepresented inn . . . least of all the innkeeper. With that said, it should be noted that no fees were charged to be listed in this book.

We've joked about starting a respite care service for innkeepers. Their hours are long, and during busy seasons their breaks are few. We share a deep respect for them and for their pioneering spirit in this growing Michigan industry. Their concern for your comfort and their dedication to preserving a part of this state's history enriches us all.

You will notice that we deliberately did not include directions to each lodging. Our experience is that most innkeepers have become very adept at guiding guests in and out of their city and can make immediate adjustments in their routes to contend with construction projects and road changes. Several have also printed maps in their brochures. Throw in a couple stops at "almost there" gas stations and you should not have any trouble finding your way at all!

The Inns

Superior 9–29

Bogan Lane Inn, Mackinac Island
Colonial House Inn and Motel,
  St. Ignace
Haan Cottage, Mackinac Island
Helmer House Inn, McMillan
House of Ludington, Escanaba
Marina Guest House, Manistique
Stonecliffe, Mackinac Island

Land of Little Bays 31–90

Apple Beach Inn, Northport
Bay Bed and Breakfast, Charlevoix
Bed and Breakfast of Ludington,
  Ludington
Brookside Inn, Beulah
Chimney Corners, Frankfort
Country Cottage, Maple City
E. E. Douville Bed and Breakfast,
  Manistee
Fireside Inn, Alpena
Gulls' Way, Petoskey
Harbour Inn on the Bay, Harbor
  Springs
The House on the Hill, Ellsworth
Leelanau Country Inn, Maple City
Neahtawanta Inn, Traverse City
  (Bowers Harbor)
The Old Mill Pond Inn, Northport
The Patchwork Parlour
  Bed'n'Breakfast, Charlevoix
Plum Lane Inn, Northport
The Riverside Inn, Leland
Stafford's Bay View Inn, Petoskey
Walloon Lake Inn, Walloon Lake
  Village
Warwickshire Inn, Traverse City
Windermere Inn, Beulah
Wood How Lodge, Northport

The Southern Shore 91–137

Gordon Beach Inn, Union Pier
Hidden Pond Farm, Fennville
The Inn at Union Pier, Union Pier
Kemah Guest House, Saugatuck
The Kirby House, Saugatuck
The Last Resort, South Haven
Morning Glory Inn, Montague
The Park House, Saugatuck

The Parsonage 1915, Holland
Pebble House, Lakeside
Pentwater Inn, Pentwater
Rosemont Inn, Douglas
Singapore Country Inn, Saugatuck
The Stagecoach Stop, Lamont
Stonegate Inn Bed and Breakfast,
  Nunica
Wickwood Inn, Saugatuck
The Winchester Inn, Allegan
Yesterday's Inn Bed and Breakfast,
  Niles

Heartland 139–86

Blue Lake Lodge, Mecosta
Chaffin Farms Bed and Breakfast,
  Ithaca
Clifford Lake Hotel, Stanton
Grist Mill Guest House, Homer
Hall House Bed and Breakfast,
  Kalamazoo
Hansen's Guest House, Homer
McCarthy's Bear Creek Inn, Marshall
The Mendon Country Inn, Mendon
Mulberry House, Owosso
Munro House Bed and Breakfast,
  Jonesville
National House Inn, Marshall
Osceola Inn, Reed City
River Haven, White Pigeon
Rosewood Country Inn, Adrian
The Shack Country Inn, White Cloud
Stuart Avenue Inn, Kalamazoo
Victorian Villa, Union City

Metro 187–221

The Botsford Inn, Farmington Hills
The Garfield Inn, Port Austin
Governor's Inn, Lexington
The Homestead, Saline
Lake Street Manor, Port Austin
Mayflower Hotel, Plymouth
Montague Inn, Saginaw
Murphy Inn, St. Clair
Oakbrook Inn, Davison
Raymond House Inn, Port Sanilac
Vickie Van's Bed and Breakfast,
  Lexington
The Victorian Inn, Port Huron

SUPERIOR

McMillan

Manistique   St. Ignace   Mackinac Island

Escanaba

Harbor Springs

Petoskey
Charlevoix
Ellsworth   Walloon Lake Village
Northport
Leland   Alpena
Maple City   Bowers Harbor
Traverse City
Frankfort   Beulah

LAND OF LITTLE BAYS

Manistee   Port Austin

Ludington
   Reed City
Pentwater THE

SOUTHERN   Mecosta
     White Cloud   Saginaw   Port Sanilac
Montague   Stanton   Frankenmuth
SHORE   Ithaca   Lexington

Davison
Nunica   Lamont   Owosso   Port Huron
   Grand Rapids   St. Clair

Holland   Lansing   METRO
Saugatuck
Douglas   Fennville   HEARTLAND   Farmington Hills
     Allegan   Plymouth   Detroit
South Haven   Dearborn
    Kalamazoo   Marshall
          Saline
      Homer
Lakeside   Mendon   Union City   Jonesville
Union Pier   Adrian
    Niles   White Pigeon

Bogan Lane Inn, *Mackinac Island*
Colonial House Inn and Motel, *St. Ignace*
Haan Cottage, *Mackinac Island*
Helmer House Inn, *McMillan*
House of Ludington, *Escanaba*
Marina Guest House, *Manistique*
Stonecliffe, *Mackinac Island*

Superior

Bogan Lane Inn
Mackinac Island

Patricia Martin's bed-and-breakfast home was built around 1858 by Mackinac Island resident Frank Bogan. Located on a tiny, steep side street just half a block from the lake, the two-story frame house was occupied by Frank and his wife until their deaths several decades later. The history of this house is rather sketchy because there are no known records on the structure or property from the mid-1850s to the middle of this century. What information there is indicates that the home was abandoned in about 1916 and sat empty for more than forty years until Charles G. Brown bought the place in 1957.

It had become known as the Haunted House, although Trish claims that anything left abandoned on the island for very long becomes

"haunted!" Photos taken in 1959 show it as an eerie-looking cottage with Virginia creeper crawling up the sides and devouring the porch. Brown worked with several other island friends to make the cottage bright and solid again. He also built on a two-story, south-facing porch addition.

Trish and her family moved into the home in 1964 and lived there year-round for nine years. When her parents moved off the island in 1973, Trish left to attend Alma College, but the family retained ownership of the home. About the same time that her need for a summer job became apparent, Trish stayed at a guesthouse in Stratford, Ontario, and became inspired to follow suit. In 1977, she opened Bogan Lane Inn for summer bed-and-breakfast lodging.

Bogan Lane Inn has four sleeping rooms, all bright, airy, and quite pretty. Many of the furnishings, including wooden bedsteads and dressers, are from the family's collection of antiques. Attached to one of the second floor rooms is a screened porch that beckons the glorious lake breezes and can be used as a sitting area or additional sleeping room. The setup is perfect for people traveling with children.

Guests are encouraged to use the main-floor living room—also filled with family antiques—and the front porch is a great place to while away some time watching the goings on of this busy island. Breakfast is served at a large table in the dining room and features pastries and baked goods fresh and hot from Trish's kitchen.

There are rumors about what it is like to spend a winter on Mackinac Island. Ask Trish to tell you some stories—she spent ten winters there on Bogan Street and attended the island school where she now teaches. She has an obvious love for the island and a deep, knowledgeable appreciation of its history and traditions. You will understand after talking to her that, to a devoted resident, the island's true magic lies well beyond Main Street.

Vitals

rooms: 4 sleeping rooms that share 2 full bathrooms

children: yes, roll-aways and cribs are available

pets: no

smoking: not inside the house

open season: May 15 through Labor Day, winter accommodations may be possible, contact the innkeeper

rates: $40 double occupancy, $7 extra person

rates include: Continental breakfast

owners: the Martin family

innkeeper:
Patricia Martin
P.O. Box 482
Mackinac Island, MI 49757
(906) 847-3439

Colonial House Inn and Motel
St. Ignace

The original two-story section of the Colonial House Inn was built as a private home more than 115 years ago by Irish immigrant John Chambers. Chambers came from Ireland in 1846 and settled on Mackinac Island in 1849. Twenty years later, he moved his family to St. Ignace and built the dwelling on State Street, overlooking Moran Bay. Even then its location was prominent, and the Chambers prospered in the town. Son Michael became a state representative and served as mayor of St. Ignace. In 1910, the children, quite grown by then, had the stately Colonial Revival addition built onto the front of the old family home as a tribute to their successes.

John Routhier, who was captain of the ore ships for International Harvester, bought the building in the mid-1940s with his wife Lenore, who operated it as a commercial lodging establishment for nearly thirty years. When the captain died, Mrs. Routhier began to phase out the

business and eventually locked the doors behind her, leaving most of the furnishings. For several years, it sat abandoned.

Everell Fisher, Jr., bought and renovated the structure in 1981. He plastered, papered, and painted—putting a halt to the old home's rapid decline. Three years later, Joel and Ailene Wittstein, while vacationing in the Upper Peninsula, learned that the inn was for sale and were hooked as soon as they saw it. They canceled plans to move to Colorado and left their home in Union Lake bound, instead, for St. Ignace.

"When we bought the place, all the beds and most of the dressers were here," explained Ailene. "Our accessories fit beautifully . . . all the bed linens we'd been saving, the antique pillow cases, the dresser sets, and pictures . . . we've been able to use them all!"

The inn is filled with a fascinating collection of antique furniture representing various periods and previous owners. The two sleeping rooms located in the oldest wing of the second floor are cozy and sweetly informal. A large old honey-colored spinning wheel sits in one as though still waiting for its mistress spinner. The three sleeping rooms in the turn-of-the-century addition are larger and more elegantly fur-

nished. A massive bedroom set that belonged to Captain Routhier dominates the master suite and is set off handsomely by framed Great Lakes navigational charts on the walls.

The view from the second-floor porch looks out over the harbor and up and down State Street. Directly across the street are the Arnold and Star boat lines that will take you to magical Mackinac Island, visible on the horizon.

Ailene and Joel are delighted to host guests bringing children, and they have set up a Colonial arts and crafts room where kids can both play and learn at the same time. They have also opened a small shop in the inn that sells fine handcrafted items made by some of their guests.

Next to the inn is a twelve-unit motel, added in the late 1950s by Captain and Mrs. Routhier. Those who prefer a private bath and more conventional lodging may be more comfortable there. Motel guests are welcome to join those in the main house for coffee or tea in the living room anytime between 7:30 A.M. and 11:00 P.M. Guests of the inn are served an extended Continental breakfast set with silver and china. For special occasions it will be served in bed.

Vitals

rooms: 5 in the inn that share 2 full baths; 12 with private baths in the adjacent motel

children: yes, encouraged

pets: no

smoking: in the motel only

open season: motel is open June 1 through Labor Day, inn is open year-round

rates: $30 through $48

rates include: Continental breakfast for inn guests

owners/innkeepers:
Joel and Ailene Wittstein
90 North State Street
St. Ignace, MI 49781
(906) 643-6900

Haan Cottage
Mackinac Island

By the time Joyce and Vernon Haan bought the old Greek Revival–style house next to Ste. Anne's Catholic Church, it had been vacant for fifteen years and was in very poor shape. But the Haans looked beyond its crumbling state and felt it was worth saving. They spent a few weeks each summer for several years rebuilding foundations and walls and discovering the history of their island home.

Haan Cottage is listed in the bicentennial registry as the oldest Greek Revival building in the Northwest Territory. The main section of the home was constructed in 1830, and it rests on the foundation of a log cabin that existed sometime in the late eighteenth century. The west wing, with its distinctive two-story porch, was added around 1847.

Sometime several years after the house was built, it became the family residence of Colonel William Preston. Preston was an officer at Fort Mackinac and served as mayor of Mackinac Island during the first

two decades of this century. The last known resident of the house, prior to the Haans' purchasing it, was Preston's daughter Margaret.

Among the treasures discovered by Joyce and Vernon during the restoration process were an 1817 gold sovereign and an 1847 newspaper, which helped date the addition. Vernon also unearthed several bones he thought might have belonged to a deer until he uncovered two moccasins. An archaeologist verified that the remains were those of an Indian woman, so they were carefully replaced in the centuries-old grave under the kitchen. Joyce explained that early Indians often brought their dead to Mackinac Island for burial because they felt it was a "special place."

When the restoration of the historic pillared structure was completed in the spring of 1984, Vernon and Joyce turned it over to Mary Ellen Jerstrom and it was opened as a bed-and-breakfast lodging.

"It's restful and peaceful here," said Mary Ellen, "and so out of the ordinary. Being in this house is like going back to a moment in time."

All of the rooms are furnished with Victorian and Early American antiques. Some were in the house when the Haans acquired it, such as

the writing desk Colonel Preston used at the fort. But most of the pieces were hand-picked by the Haans, and many have their own interesting history. One example is a pair of twin cannonball beds. The oldest was built in 1790 and is still outfitted with a horsehair mattress. The newer bed is a reproduction built 70 years later—making it still more than 150 years old!

Mary Ellen serves a home-baked Continental breakfast in the first-floor parlor of the original wing. From the front porches, her guests can watch the horse-drawn carriages and wagons that transport food and supplies as well as visitors around the island. The bay is directly across the street, and just a few minutes walk to the west are the historic fort and business district.

Vitals

rooms: 6 sleeping rooms, 4 have private baths; an efficiency with a private bath, kitchen, living room, and 2 full-size sleepers is also available

children: yes

pets: no

smoking: yes

open season: May 15 through October 15

rates: $50 through $85 per room for two, one- and two-bedroom suites are $165 and $245, discounts for off-season

rates include: Continental breakfast

owners: Vernon and Joyce Haan

innkeeper:

Mary Ellen Jerstrom
P.O. Box 1268
Mackinac Island, MI 49757
(906) 847-3403

Helmer House Inn
McMillan

More than one hundred years ago, the Reverend Mills, a Presbyterian minister, came to the shores of Big Manistique Lake and built a mission house to help accommodate early settlers. In 1887, Gale Helmer purchased the mission and converted it into a successful lakeside resort and general store. The area became a center of activity. It was a convenient halfway point between Curtis and McMillan, and the stagecoach and mail wagon stopped there.

When the federal government designated the site as a post office in 1904, they appointed Mr. Helmer postmaster and officially gave the four-corners his name. That same year, Charles and Jeanie Fyvie, who had earlier immigrated from Scotland, arrived in Helmer. They bought the resort and Charles took over as postmaster. The resort business thrived for several years.

As the 1950s were ushered in, the glorious days of clapboard resorts and dance pavilions were coming to an end, and the scene at Helmer was changing drastically. The general store had closed. The old lodge and homestead were deteriorating and eventually abandoned.

Responsibility for the building fell to Rob Goldthorpe, grandson of the Fyvies, and one of three grandchildren to have been born at the old homestead. Faced with the choice of tearing down the building or fixing it, Rob and his wife Marge embarked on a complete renovation of the structure and reopened the Helmer House in 1982.

Like traditional old roadside inns, Helmer House has both a restaurant and sleeping quarters. The dining room seating is located where the wraparound porch once stretched along the front and south side of the house. The area is now enclosed and each table sits by a large window. Around the corner from the dining area is the living room where dinner patrons can wait for a table and overnight guests mingle among plush, overstuffed Victorian-era couches and family heirlooms.

The second- and third-floor sleeping rooms vary in size and are all furnished with lovely antiques. Fine old iron, brass, and wooden bedsteads come complete with thick feather comforters for cold U.P. nights. Turn-of-the-century memorabilia decorate the rooms, and each has a dresser so you can unpack and stay for awhile. Take a look at the many

clocks that adorn the walls throughout the inn. They are from an extensive private collection that was gathered over several years.

Innkeeper Marion Schroeder has lived in the Upper Peninsula for twenty-five years and she knows the area well. She can point you to the best swimming ("around the corner") and cross-country skiing ("just across the road") and will furnish you with local maps for other outdoor activities. She oversees all kitchen operations and gives attentive care to the guests.

The inn has a well-deserved reputation for good food. We enjoyed a superb whitefish dinner and were greeted the next morning with steaming French toast and fresh fruit. A full breakfast is served to all overnight guests. The dining room is open to the public for lunch and dinner Wednesday through Monday.

The Reverend Mills probably never dreamed that his simple frame mission house would play such a big part in the development of the town that was to follow, nor that it would so graciously enter its second century.

Vitals

rooms: 5 sleeping rooms that share a full bath on the second floor
and a water closet on the third; 3 rooms have vanities with sinks

children: yes

pets: no

smoking: yes in dining room, discouraged in sleeping rooms

open season: April through November

rates: $25 through $40 per room, double occupancy

rates include: full breakfast

owners: Robert and Marge Goldthorpe

innkeeper:

Marion Schroeder
County Road 417
McMillan, MI 49853
(906) 586-3204

House of Ludington
Escanaba

"I always liked this place," remembers Gerald Lancour, owner of the House of Ludington. And in the past century, so have thousands of others. The Atlantic City–style hotel at the foot of Ludington Street, on Little Bay de Noc, has courted travelers since 1868. Additions put on during the first few decades of its life brought the hotel's offerings to one hundred sleeping rooms and a livery stable for guests' horses.

Chicago businessman Pat Hayes bought the hotel in 1939. He was a flamboyant character and did much to perpetuate and enhance the House of Ludington's reputation for class and style. In 1959, he installed an exterior glass-walled elevator running up the front of the hotel, which gave guests an outstanding view of the bay as they ascended to their rooms. National and international personalities, stars, politicians, and figures from the underworld made the House of Ludington their home away from home.

In later years, as the economic climate and ownership changed, the

building grew old and business dropped. By the early 1980s, the hotel was vacant and deteriorating fast.

Gerald, his wife Vernice, and a sister-in-law and brother-in-law, were looking for a business to get into after retirement. They had planned to head for Florida until the forlorn old hotel caught Gerald's eye. Judging by its state of disrepair, he felt that he was looking at the last opportunity to save it, and he couldn't turn it down.

Their initial and most major renovation took three months and was masterful to say the least. The hotel is once again a proud landmark, a center of activity with the park and bay shore just across the street. And it is an enjoyable place to stay. All of the sleeping rooms have been individually redecorated in styles from contemporary to traditional. Some are furnished with original hotel pieces such as a matching bed and dresser with tiny, hand-painted, porcelain drawer pulls, each featuring a different scene. The rooms have private bathrooms and air-conditioning, and they are spotlessly clean and quiet. Many of the smaller rooms have been combined to make larger rooms and suites with

sitting areas, and guests still ride the famous glass elevator to get to their floor.

Meals are served with linen and fine table service in two elegant rooms on the main floor. The King George dining room has a very large, original fireplace with priceless silver and china from the hotel's early days displayed on its hearth and in beautiful old glass cases. Some of the original place settings are still used. The waiters are formally attired and they serve at a slow, easy pace so diners can relax and feel unrushed. Our orders of kastler ripchen and Wiener schnitzel were superb, and the whole dining experience remains a very pleasant memory.

Gerald and Vernice bought out their partners and now run the hotel side by side. Vernice's decorating talents and her eye for detail can be seen throughout the hotel, but an encapsulated sampling is her creation of a miniature Victorian home on display in the lobby. The project took three years to complete and could hold your attention for hours. Take a look at it and see if you can figure out who ended up with the piece of cake missing from the pantry.

A high level of quality is apparent in every aspect of this historic hotel, as is warm hospitality from the people who work there.

Vitals

rooms: 23 with private baths

children: yes

pets: up to discretion of innkeeper

smoking: yes

open season: year-round

rates: $36 through $40 double occupancy; $55 for small suites

rates include: room only

owners/innkeepers:
  Gerald and Vernice Lancour
  223 Ludington Street
  Escanaba, MI 49829
  (906) 786-4000

Marina Guest House
Manistique

From Margaret Beach's home, guests can see the Manistique marina and lighthouse, focal points in this Lake Michigan harbor town. The large house was built in 1905 by a lawyer whose estate at one time extended to the water. An addition was put on in 1922. According to Margaret, it served as a bed-and-breakfast home during the 1920s, and Swedish pancakes were a specialty there. Margaret acquired the home in October, 1983, and opened soon after for guests. She recently retired from twenty-seven years of teaching.

There are six comfortable bedrooms located on the second and third floors. Guests are also welcome to use the living room, dining room, and sun room on the first floor. Often they will join Margaret to watch TV or sit and visit. The living room fireplace is ready for stoking on chilly Upper Peninsula nights. Margaret has taken classes in French cuisine, pastry, and garde-manger. She serves a substantial breakfast to all her guests.

Vitals

rooms: 6 upstairs sleeping rooms that share 3 half baths

children: by reservation only

pets: no

smoking: no

open season: May 1 through November 1

rates: $25 single, $35 double, special rates for children

rates include: full breakfast

owner/innkeeper:

Margaret Beach
230 Arbutus
P.O. Box 344
Manistique, MI 49854
(906) 341-5147

Stonecliffe
Mackinac Island

On a cool summer evening, we caught a 10:30 horse-drawn carriage at Mackinac Island's waterfront and settled back for the twenty-minute trek to Stonecliffe. This magnificent English Tudor mansion sits high on the west bluff of the island. It is the focal point of a 175-acre estate built in 1904 as a summer residence for the Michael Cudahy family of Chicago and Milwaukee. According to Eugene T. Peterson, former superintendent of the Mackinac Island State Park Commission, the home set a standard of opulence unequaled in the island's history. Its total cost to build, in those early years of the new century, was $35,000.

Michael Cudahy died just a few years after completion of the mansion, and it was then sold to Mr. A. T. Herdt who made his fortune by

holding the patent on creosote. Herdt also passed away soon after acquiring the home, but his widow retained ownership and spent summers there until after World War II.

Upon her death, the estate was willed to the Episcopalian Church and later donated to Moral Re-Armament (MRA). The activities of MRA on Mackinac Island lasted from 1945 to 1968. Evangelist Rex Humbard took over the estate from 1969 to 1977, when George Staffan purchased it and opened the Tudor home as an inn.

Most of the mansion's fourteen sleeping rooms are very large and are appointed with some of the original Victorian and Empire furnishings as well as king- and queen-sized beds. Cudahy's library on the first floor is still filled with his books, and the Great Room has a hand-carved marble fireplace that decades ago was obtained from the Italian pavilion at the Chicago World's Fair.

One of Stonecliffe's greatest attractions is its tranquility. Tucked in a clearing in the woods, far away from the bustle of town, Stonecliffe offers acres of beautiful grounds for walking and plenty of quiet. There

is a striking view of the Straits from the Italianate veranda—especially impressive at sunset. Even during the busiest tourist seasons, Stonecliffe maintains the peacefulness that first beckoned wealthy industrialists to the island.

Stonecliffe's restaurant is located on the grounds in a lodge built by Herdt. Recent additions to the estate include a pool and several Tudor-style condominiums that are available for overnight accommodations. If you have a preference for staying in the condominiums or the mansion, be sure to specify when making reservations.

Cars are not permitted on Mackinac Island, but horse-drawn carriages will transport guests from the boat docks to the estate, one and one-half miles inland. Special seasonal Stonecliffe shuttles run several times each day, also. Ask the innkeeper for a schedule. Bicycles are available, and the year-round state-maintained airstrip borders the Stonecliffe grounds.

Vitals

rooms: 14 in the mansion; 52 condominium units; specify if you have a preference, all have private baths

children: yes

pets: no

smoking: yes

open season: May 1 through January 2

rates: $60 through $135 in the mansion, $80 through $185 in the condominiums, all double occupancy; spring and fall packages available

rates include: room only

owner/innkeeper:
George Staffan
P.O. Box 338
Mackinac Island, MI 49757
(906) 847-3355

Apple Beach Inn, *Northport*
Bay Bed and Breakfast, *Charlevoix*
Bed and Breakfast of Ludington, *Ludington*
Brookside Inn, *Beulah*
Chimney Corners, *Frankfort*
Country Cottage, *Maple City*
E. E. Douville Bed and Breakfast, *Manistee*
Fireside Inn, *Alpena*
Gulls' Way, *Petoskey*
Harbour Inn on the Bay, *Harbor Springs*
The House on the Hill, *Ellsworth*
Leelanau Country Inn, *Maple City*
Neahtawanta Inn, *Traverse City (Bowers Harbor)*
The Old Mill Pond Inn, *Northport*
The Patchwork Parlour Bed'n'Breakfast, *Charlevoix*
Plum Lane Inn, *Northport*
The Riverside Inn, *Leland*
Stafford's Bay View Inn, *Petoskey*
Walloon Lake Inn, *Walloon Lake Village*
Warwickshire Inn, *Traverse City*
Windermere Inn, *Beulah*
Wood How Lodge, *Northport*

Land of Little Bays

Apple Beach Inn
Northport

Apple Beach Inn sits well back from the main road and is surrounded by mature maples, fruit trees, and patches of meadow. It was built as a private home in 1860 by a wealthy St. Louis family whose many interests included raising Morgan horses. "The family was quite fancy," the home's present owner, Mary Anne Taylor, told us. "I like to think about what I might have been wearing if I were here with them one hundred years ago, perhaps making my way up from the beach in a long dress and a bustle."

Mary Anne saw the home while on vacation in 1965 and was drawn to it immediately. She says simply, "I had to have it." It became the Taylors' summer home and might have remained so were it not for Mary Anne's mother, Bea Bowen, owner of the Plum Lane Inn just up the hill. Mary Anne began by taking some of Plum Lane's overflow or an occasional overbooking. She enjoyed it so much that she opened of-

ficially in early summer 1985. Like nearly all the innkeepers we have talked with, Mary Anne said the joy of owning a bed-and-breakfast home is the guests. "They're like gifts," she explains. "They are the pivotal part of the whole experience."

Strong, clean lines and bright rooms characterize this fine old summer home. The living room has the front entry at one end and the back door at the other, a classic shotgun-style room—long and straight, and positoned to catch the lake breezes. The maple floor, white walls, and wicker and caned furniture enhance its cool, summery feeling. Off the living room, facing the lake, is a large, lovely sleeping room with a fireplace, private bath, and screen porch. Two smaller sleeping rooms on the second floor are papered with pretty print wallpaper and share a bath with a larger, dormitory-style room.

Breakfast is served in a sunny dining room. Our meal included a rich cheese quiche, hot cinnamon and walnut muffins, and a fresh fruit bowl garnished with mint that Mary Anne had picked near the beach that morning. On other days, the choices might include pancakes with

maple syrup or a Pinconning cheese omelet. Soft classical music often plays in the background. Through the dining room's tall bay window you can look out onto a field of wildflowers and young trees, and beyond them to the blue waters of Traverse Bay.

The shore is edged with the old apple orchards that gave rise to the inn's name. A walking path will take you from the porch of the inn to the beach, where you will find a gazebo at the water's edge. It is very private and quiet—a delightful place to sip wine or lemonade in the late afternoon. Mary Anne joined us for coffee there the next morning and we watched the sun rise across the bay.

Even on cool, gray, rainy days, the lake and rolling surf have a mesmerizing quality that can hold our attention for hours. But should you find yourself at Apple Beach Inn on a dreary day and not so entranced by the lake, you will find ample good reading material and a fireplace to warm chilled bones. The town's shops and restaurants are within walking distance.

Vitals

rooms: 4, 1 with private bath

children: by special arrangement

pets: no

smoking: on porch or outside only

open season: summer and fall

rates: $55 through $80 double occupancy

rates include: breakfast

owner/innkeeper:

Mary Anne Taylor
617 Shabwasung (M-22), Box 2
Northport, MI 49670
(616) 386-5022

Bay Bed and Breakfast
Charlevoix

On a warm summer afternoon in late July, we sipped iced tea with Marian Taylor-Beatty on the sixty-by-fourteen-foot deck of her bed-and-breakfast home overlooking Lake Michigan. The lake was very still, and Marian noted that it was a good day for floating on an inner tube. Marian knows the lake well. She and her husband Jack bought this home in the late 1960s while they were living in Mount Pleasant, and in the mid-1970s they moved in full-time. In 1984, they began offering lodging to bed and breakfast travelers.

The house sits atop a small bluff and is nestled in a woods of mature hemlock and hardwoods just fifty to sixty feet from the beach. Two sleeping rooms are available. The Tree Trunk Room on the first floor is furnished with a high wooden bedstead and is adjacent to the shared bathroom. The second floor Tree Top Room is reached by a spiral staircase from the living room. It has windows all around that give the room the feel of a private, well-decorated tree house. A large expanse of glass that reaches from the living room floor to its cathedral ceiling offers a spectacular view of the lake. There are scores of books to read and a cozy wood-burning stove for cold days.

Breakfast is ample and might include eggs Benedict Blackstone, which has the addition of a sautéed sliced tomato, or specialty pancakes with almonds. Smoked salmon from Marian's hometown of Newport, Oregon, is also often available.

The sandy shore beckons those who like to swim or beachcomb, and there is a lifetime supply of great skipping stones. Guests may also use Jack and Marian's canoe and inner tubes. Downhill and cross-country skiing are offered nearby for those looking for winter fun. The home is secluded and quiet, and just twelve miles from Charlevoix.

Vitals

rooms: 2 that share 1 bath

children: over 12 years of age

pets: no

smoking: outside only

open season: year-round

rates: $52 and $62 double occupancy

rates include: breakfast

owners/innkeepers:

Jackson and Marian Taylor-Beatty
Route 1, Box 136A
Charlevoix, MI 49720
(616) 599-2570

Bed and Breakfast of Ludington
Ludington

Grace and Robert Schneider's home is nestled on fifteen acres in Good Creek Valley, just four miles from Ludington. It is surrounded by seventy acres of state land, and it is a paradise for people seeking the rest and relaxation that comes with spending time in the out-of-doors. The Schneiders' home is very comfortable and nicely furnished, but, said Robert, "The real beauty is outside these walls." On a warm summer afternoon, he loaned us each a cap and took us for a walk.

We started across the street through a forest of mature beech and conifers, following Good Creek, which ran crystal clear over a sandy bottom. I took off my shoes and waded for several yards—it was years since I had enjoyed that most delectable and simple of pleasures. Later, we headed up through the meadow behind the house to a ridge that overlooks the valley. From that vantage, it is easy to see how the area is well protected from northerly winds. That protection and the abundance of fresh water are good clues as to why the Potawatami settled there during the 1800s.

During the summer, there are black and red raspberries for the picking, as well as strawberries, currants, and blueberries. Robert also showed us a series of small ponds, fed by Good Creek, that he keeps stocked with Rocky Mountain spotted rainbow trout. There is a picnic area, plenty of room for outdoor games, and good bird-watching. In winter, there are toboggans and snowshoes that guests may use at no additional charge, and cross-country skis may be rented nearby. There is also a Jacuzzi to soak away any last cares.

The Schneiders enjoy having families visit. Children are welcome and a crib is available. Breakfast is served daily. Snacks and hot and cold drinks are usually offered during the day. In addition to their innkeeping responsibilities, Grace is a nurse and Robert is part lumberjack, carpenter, mason, and gardener. They are a warm, earnest couple, and they enjoy sharing the pleasures of Good Creek Valley.

Vitals

rooms: 5 that share 3 baths

children: yes

pets: yes

smoking: outside only

open season: year-round

rates: $28 single, $32 through $38 double, $6 per extra occupant in same room

rates include: breakfast

owners/innkeepers:
  Grace and Robert Schneider
  2458 South Beaune Road
  Ludington, MI 49431
  (616) 843-9768

Brookside Inn
Beulah

When Pam Powell and Kirk Lorenz began creating the Brookside Inn, they used a pretty basic formula. Said Kirk, "We just put in the things we liked and omitted what we disliked!"

You will find that what they like, for example, are king-sized water beds housed in custom-made wooden frames with lovely etched mirrors in the canopy. Some of the beds have softly lighted glass display cases built into the headboards. Then Pam and Kirk added private bathrooms and equipped each with a hair dryer, curling iron, and the thickest six-foot-long towels they could find. They also included in each room a remote control TV, a small wood-burning stove, and a built-in Polynesian spa with temperature and water-jet controls.

The rooms are individually decorated around differing themes and have been given names instead of numbers. In the New Orleans Room,

wrought iron window trim and flower boxes give the flavor of old Bourbon Street. The wallpaper in the Garden Room looks like a continuous watercolor painting of flowers, and the Victorian Room is furnished with lacy pillows, fans trimmed with ribbons and flowers, and an old marble-topped vanity—very classy and very complete.

About the only reason for guests to leave their rooms is for meals, but Kirk and Pam have taken care of that, too. The main floor of the inn is a restaurant furnished with antiques, collectibles, and all manner of country memorabilia. Large windows at the back of the dining room look out onto a tree-sheltered wooden patio surrounded by quiet Eden Brook and nestled among tall wildflowers. It is a favored spot for dining during pleasant weather, and it is frequently visited by small wildlife

looking for leftovers. Beyond the deck are herb gardens from which come many of the seasonings for the daily fare.

The restaurant is open to the public all day long, and baked goods produced from the kitchen long before sunup can be purchased from a glass case in the lobby. All of the food is homemade—"from scratch." Overnight guests check in early enough to partake of dinner, which is included with the room, as is a full breakfast.

In 1983, Kirk and Pam opened the Hotel Frankfort, a lovely Victorian-style structure in its namesake city, with accommodations similar to those at the Brookside. Reservations for either may be made by calling the Brookside.

Vitals

rooms: 15 with private bath, Polynesian spa, king-sized canopied water bed; rooms with saunas, steam baths, and tanning solariums also available

children: no

pets: no

smoking: yes

open season: year-round

rates: $145 through $250

rates include: dinner and breakfast for two, all taxes and tips; alcohol *not* included

owners/innkeepers:
Kirk Lorenz and Pam Powell
115 North Michigan Avenue
Beulah, MI 49617
(616) 882-7271

Chimney Corners
Frankfort

Chimney Corners has been a Rogers family operation from the very beginning. The Rogers brothers came to the Crystal Lake area about 1910. They were partners in the Piqua Handle Company and bought up forty- and eighty-acre parcels of land to log the hardwood. They were particularly fond of a large wooded tract of land that bordered the north shore of the lake, so they built a log cabin there. During the Depression, they moved onto the land permanently, added rooms to the cabin, and began to take in boarders. Mother Rogers's family had been involved with resorts in the Poconos so innkeeping came easy to her. As business increased, the men built a cottage on the property and rented it, then they built another . . . today there are eighteen!

Son Jim and his wife Mollie took over the running of Chimney Corners during the 1950s. Their daughter, Claudia, and her husband

Rick Herman now do much of the work assisted by *their* children.

You cannot see the old log lodge from the highway, but it is easily reached by following a winding wooded road, well-marked on Crystal Drive. The lodge is still in daily use throughout the summer, and in the oldest section you can see the original time-worn-smooth log walls. The main floor has a cozy sitting room loaded with books and two lovely dining rooms that serve some of the best food around. Diners are offered the difficult choice of such items as duck à l'orange, charbroiled ribeye steaks, and broiled whitefish served amid the warmth of stone fireplaces and family tradition. Simple country fare! The restaurant is open to the public, and its success over the years prompted Mollie to publish a cookbook called *There's Always Something Cooking at Chimney Corners,* now in its second edition.

On the second floor of the lodge are small, cottagelike sleeping rooms with dormers and rough wood walls. The furnishings are simple and comfortable with here-and-there an occassional brass bed or handsome wooden dresser. Guests in the eight rooms share two bathrooms.

On the main floor, accessible from a separate entrance, is a small apartment with a private bath, a fireplace, and a great view of the lake. I lost count of the number of fireplaces in the lodge but did learn that the innkeepers' Aunt Nancy built several of them—as well as many of those in the eighteen cottages and five lakeside apartments.

Breakfast and lunch are served at the beach dining room located on a narrow strip of land between the road and Crystal Lake. It is very casual and offers a spectacular and weather-protected view of the water and Chimney Corners' thousand feet of beach.

Vitals

rooms: 9 in lodge; 8 rooms share 2 baths; 1 room has a private bath, large sitting area and a fireplace; also available are 18 cottages and 5 apartments

children: yes

pets: up to discretion of innkeeper

smoking: lodge, preferably outside and on porches; cabins, yes

open season: May through October

rates: $25 through $45

rates include: use of beach and tennis facilities

owners/innkeepers:

Mollie and Jim Rogers
Claudia and Rick Herman
1602 Crystal Drive
Frankfort, MI 49635
(616) 352-7522

Country Cottage
Maple City

Karen Eitzen grew up around Maple City on her family's fruit farm, part of the land originally homesteaded by her great-grandfather. She has an extensive background in the hospitality industry and now manages a restaurant in the area. Karen spent seven years in Florence, Italy, teaching physical education, and later moved into the international gold and silver jewelry market in Tel Aviv. She speaks fluent Italian and Hebrew.

Karen's split-level bed-and-breakfast home was built in the mid-1970s. She offers guests three second-floor sleeping rooms and a comfortable living room with a color TV. The decor is contemporary with a country influence. Her living quarters are in a wing off the kitchen, affording both guests and innkeeper as much privacy as they want. Guests who rent the whole house may also have use of the kitchen. Flower gardens and lots of bird feeders can be found around the yard, and a back deck and picnic table beckon Karen's guests to enjoy the outdoors. A large locked garage is available for those traveling by bicycle.

The location is good for both summer and winter activities. Lake Michigan and Sugar Loaf are one and one-half miles away, and the Leelanau Country Inn is just next door for dining and cocktails. Karen's breakfast includes baked goods, cereal, hard-cooked eggs, and dry cereals. As an added touch, she keeps on hand extra shampoo and other toiletries for guests who forget to bring their own.

Vitals

rooms: 3

children: ask the innkeeper

pets: no

smoking: common areas and outside only

open season: year-round

rates: $40 to $45 per room, $125 for the whole house

rates include: breakfast

owner/innkeeper:
Karen J. Eitzen
135 East Harbor Highway (M-22)
Maple City, MI 49664
(616) 228-5328

E. E. Douville Bed and Breakfast
Manistee

Barbara and Bill Johnson bought their big home on Pine Street in 1978, just a year from its one hundredth birthday. It was built by E. E. Douville, a wealthy business man from Wisconsin who made his money in insurance and real estate. According to Bill, Douville's name appeared frequently in the society columns of the local paper, and he liked to "hobnob with all the lumber barons." He also served as mayor of the town for at least one term. But in the late 1880s, Douville left the area, and little is known about his later years.

It was Douville's generous use of pine woodwork that first attracted Barb and Bill to the house. All the windows and doors on the main floor are trimmed in wide pine boards with elaborate spoon carvings. Original interior pine shutters cover many of the windows. A graceful wind-

ing stairway in the two-story foyer leads to the three sleeping rooms for guests on the second floor.

We stayed in the spacious front room with its tall, shuttered windows that give an air of elegance. Like the other two sleeping rooms, it is beautifully decorated with plush carpeting, country prints, antiques, and a cozy bed quilt. Collections of escutcheon plates and old kitchen tools provide a glimpse of the kinds of items that might have been around when Douville first built his home.

At the end of the hall, past the sleeping rooms, is a combination kitchen, eating area, and sitting room for overnight guests. It is furnished with white wicker and is a quiet and pleasant place to read or sit and talk with other guests. In the morning, it is set up for breakfast: fresh fruit and juice in the refrigerator, coffee or a choice of teas, and some of the best muffins we have ever eaten. The shared bath just off the kitchen has a deep footed tub adapted with a shower.

Barb and Bill maintain the first floor of the home for their own living quarters and are happy to show it to guests. Its extensive pine trim will increase your appreciation for the skills of the wood-carvers who worked on E. E. Douville's home a century ago. Within walking

distance of this home are the 1903 Ramsdell Opera House and the Manistee Historical Museum. Lake Michigan is not far, and with it, fishing and boating. Charter fishing trips and tours can also be arranged on the *Pro-Ducer* with its captain, the Johnsons' son Jerry P. Johnson, who is licensed by the U.S. Coast Guard.

Vitals

rooms: 3 sleeping rooms that share 1 bath

children: 12 years of age and over

pets: no

smoking: yes

open season: year-round

rates: $35 through $40 per room

rate includes: Continental breakfast

owners/innkeepers:

William and Barbara Johnson
111 Pine Street
Manistee, MI 49660
(616) 723-8654

Fireside Inn
Alpena

> During the years of 1906 and 1907 my mother and father boarded a group of men who were lumbering Whiskey Point. She fed from 18 to 20 men three meals a day for $3 per week and did this for two years.
>
> Mother saved $350 and started to talk to dad about building a summer hotel. Dad wasn't enthused, as his brother Joe had the Birch Hill Hotel and he did not want to compete with him. But mother and I kept at it and he finally consented to build one.
>
> The only money we had was that $350 . . . but there was lots of timber around and a portable mill at the south end of the lake. We had it ready June 22, 1909. We had eight rooms upstairs and charged $10 per week for room and board. That was big money at the time. When we opened the hotel . . . our $350 was gone but everything was paid. We didn't owe one dime. It was named the Fireside Inn because it had the second fireplace at Grand Lake.*

. . . and so began the first of decades of summer lodging at the Fireside Inn, tucked along the east shore of Grand Lake north of Alpena. Kauffman, quoted above, eventually bought the inn from his father and kept it until 1945. During the next thirty years, it changed ownership only a couple of times before Lois and Bob McConnell made their way north from the Detroit suburb of Warren and bought the inn in 1975.

The resort sprawls over seventeen acres and has 700 feet of frontage on Grand Lake. There is a lot to do if you want to be outside and active, and plenty of places to cozy yourself away if you do not. Porch sitting is a great pastime at the Fireside Inn, and oh, what a porch! As the Kauffman's business increased, father and son had added a wing of rooms to the east end of the lodge, running parallel to the lake, and they extended the wide, covered porch the full length of the wing. It is nearly 215 feet long and is now shaded by huge old cedar trees that appear as twigs in a photograph taken sometime during 1912. The sleeping rooms that open onto the porch are simply furnished with a

---

*From *My Recollections of Early Grand Lake* by George H. Kauffman. In the early 1970s George Kauffman began writing stories of early Grand Lake life in letters to his grandchildren. Son-in-law Lew Sowa encouraged him to write more, with the thought of compiling the memories in a small book so they would not be lost. The first edition written with colorful and tender firsthand details was released in 1973. Three months later, Mr. Kauffman died. We are most grateful to Mr. Sowa for permission to reprint from the book.

bed or two, a dresser, and chairs. They also have screened doors for letting in the balmy lake breezes.

Between 1940 and 1945, George Kauffman built eighteen cabins on the Fireside grounds. Sixteen of varying sizes are used to house summer guests and are furnished similarly to the lodge rooms: casual and homey. Each has a refrigerator and some come with complete cooking facilities. All but one has at least one stone fireplace.

The Fireside Room in the lodge is one of the favored gathering places. The walls are finished in half logs and are covered with historic paraphernalia and old mounted birds and mammals from the area. Most of the items have been in the room for a very long time . . . passed on from owner to owner. A player piano sits in one corner with a stack of rolls that would take a week to go through. On cool days and nights, a fire is usually ablaze in the namesake hearth. If not, guests are welcome to build one. The inn is comfortably rustic, and guests seem drawn to it, says Lois, because it is safe, quiet, and easy to get-away-from-it-all.

Breakfast and dinner are served to guests in July and August. Local

residents often make reservations and come in for dinner too. A different item is served each night, rotating such features as spaghetti, chicken, and whitefish. The roast pork supper we feasted on was delicious, and we topped it off with ice cream and homemade strawberry shortcake. Breakfast was any combination of cold or hot cereal, French toast, pancakes, eggs, sausage, juice, and coffee—plenty of food to keep guests fueled for hours.

Canoes, paddleboats, and small sailboats are available to guests at all times. Boats with motors are rented for a small fee. Guests may also bring their own. On-land facilities include a tennis court and horseshoe pit, a volleyball court, and wooded walking trails.

Vitals

rooms: 16 cabins with bathrooms; 5 sleeping rooms in lodge wing, each with private bath

children: yes, encouraged

pets: by prior arrangement

smoking: yes

open season: Memorial Day through Labor Day

rates: $21 through $27 daily per adult for rooms; $185 per adult by the week for cottages; special rates for children and for off-season lodging, including Memorial Day, Labor Day, and fall color weekends

rates include: breakfast and dinner during July and August, use of all outdoor equipment except boats with motors

owners/innkeepers:
Bob and Lois McConnell
18730 Fireside Highway
Alpena, MI 49707
(517) 595-6369

Gulls' Way
Petoskey

Early in the summer of 1984, Lynn and Ed Pater opened two sleeping rooms in their home to bed-and-breakfast guests. The name of their lodging is significant. The Paters' home sits on a small side street, about half a block off US 31, directly on Little Traverse Bay. Both of the lovely, country-furnished bedrooms and the enclosed front porch have a wide, unobstructed view of the water. On the day of our visit, about a dozen sunning gulls napped and preened on the breakwater, just fifty feet away.

Petoskey and Bay View, famous for their stunning architecture, summer activities, and fine shops, are just around the corner. In addition to a seven-day-a-week summer season, the home is open on weekends during winter, and cross-country skiers are welcome.

Vitals

rooms: 2 sleeping rooms, 1 has a private bath

children: under 10 discouraged

pets: no

smoking: porch only

open season: May through October and winter weekends

rates: $40 through $50

rates include: generous Continental breakfast

owners/innkeepers:

    Lynn and Ed Pater
    118 Boulder Lane
    Petoskey, MI 49770
    (616) 347-9891

Harbour Inn on the Bay
Harbor Springs

Tom Mooradian gestured with a broad sweep of his arm across the veranda and grounds of Harbour Inn on the Bay.

"*This* was Harbor Springs," he explained. "When this grand old inn was built in 1910 and named Ramona Park Hotel, it was the epitome of the area's wealth and elegance."

Originally built with about thirty guest rooms, the hotel welcomed visitors from Cincinnati, Chicago, and St. Louis who arrived daily in Petoskey by train. During the late 1920s, a posh casino was added as well as a forty-room wing. Like many of the northern Michigan resorts that featured gambling and attracted flashy patrons, there are rumors of shady dealings with Al Capone and the Purple Gang that continued until the 1940s when games of chance were outlawed in this state.

Harbor Springs grew and flourished, and for several years so did the Ramona Park Hotel. But age was quietly creeping in, slowly robbing the resort of her grace and hospitality. In 1979, the Mooradian family

bought the hotel, renamed it, and began a major renovation to bring it back.

Large reconstruction and decorating projects are being carried out so skillfully that you may not even notice what is original and what is new. The lobby is spacious and warmly inviting—comfortable enough to feel like a living room. Beyond it is the elegant bayside dining room, softly lighted by chandeliers. All the sleeping rooms are also being redecorated and outfitted with new bathrooms. The structure curves slightly as if to cup the shore, and most of the rooms have a wide and unobstructed view of the bay.

"Do drink the water," says Tom. It comes cold and clear from an artesian well that pumps one-half-million gallons daily. It *is* outstanding.

From the grand veranda and the expansive lawn of the inn, you can see nearly the entire length of Little Traverse Bay, straight across the water to Petoskey, and to Charlevoix at its mouth. Major improvements to the waterfront now provide guests with a wide, sandy beach and good swimming. The grounds around the inn are lovely and peaceful and graced with flower gardens throughout the summer. It all combines to give the effect of country seclusion, even though the inn is actually only a few minutes drive from downtown Harbor Springs.

Vitals

rooms: 70, each with private bath

children: yes

pets: no

smoking: yes

open season: May 1 to November 1

rates: $55 per room, single occupancy; $70 per room, double occupancy; $15.00 extra per person; tour and group rate requests are welcome

rates include: full breakfast

owner/innkeeper:
Thomas Mooradian
1157 Beach Road
P.O. Box 375 TC
Harbor Springs, MI 49740
(616) 526-2107

The House on the Hill
Ellsworth

Buster and Julie Arnim sold their interest in a Houston-based luggage company a few years ago and decided that running a bed-and-breakfast home would suit them well. They made a list of about eight features they would look for, among them a location in a resort region near fresh water and close to excellent dining. A reference to northern Michigan and its resemblance to the beautiful Hudson River Valley piqued their interest in the Great Lakes State. And when they came across an ad for a farmhouse on fifty-three and a half acres in Ellsworth, they put in an offer. It was accepted, and they closed without ever having set foot in Michigan. Their first look at the area came the following January, when Ellsworth lay under five feet of snow. Julie remembers walking through the house repeating, "I love it, I love it, I love it!" It was a gutsy move, she admits. But it has worked out just fine.

As its name implies, the house sits on a hill and overlooks a valley through which flows Lake St. Clair, part of the Chain of Lakes. The Arnims' renovation work included adding a large veranda that wraps around two sides of the house and forms a gazebo at the corner. The

view from that veranda, out across the lush valley to the sparkling water and rolling landscape of this resort area, is spectacular. The three second-floor guest rooms face the lake and have windows that take advantage of the view.

The home is decorated with a country Victorian theme, elegant but casual, with touches of art from the American West. Many of the walls are framed in beautiful border papers that set off a very comfortable blend of period furnishings. The sleeping rooms are filled with the kinds of amenities that Buster and Julie have enjoyed in their travels to bed-and-breakfast homes and have incorporated for the pleasure of their own guests. Among them are end tables and reading lights on each

side of the bed, a carafe of ice water, and a plate (a whole plate!) of chocolate mints.

Within easy walking distance of the House on the Hill are two of northern Michigan's premier restaurants, the Rowe Inn and Tapawingo. If good food is what brings you to the area, save room for Buster and Julie's country breakfasts. Ours included sausage and eggs, a rich sour cream walnut coffee cake with Julie's homemade raspberry preserves, cherry butter from nearby Rocky Top Farms, and the Arnim custom-blended cherry-berry yogurt. It was served on a set of cobalt dishes that had belonged to Julie's parents and grandparents. She has several other sets of dishes she uses, and a whole repertoire of recipes.

Be prepared here for bountiful quantities of Texas hospitality—there are few things quite as endearing—and for two delightful people who adore each other. There is laughter here, and warmth and good memory-making. We can affirm the feeling Buster expressed one summer evening as dusk was settling into the valley while we sipped wine on the veranda: "It doesn't get any better than this."

Vitals

rooms: 3 that share 1 bath

children: no

pets: no

smoking: yes

open season: first week in May through December 15

rate: $60 per room

rate includes: full breakfast, tax

owners/innkeepers:
    Julie and Buster Arnim
    Box 206, Lake Street
    Ellsworth, MI 49729
    (616) 588-6304

Leelanau Country Inn
Maple City

The Leelanau Country Inn is located about eight miles south of the town of Leland and just across the road from Little Traverse Lake. The original structure was built in 1891 and served as a stop for travelers needing food and rest. An addition was put on in 1895 and the clientele began to shift to vacationers who came to the area for summer recreation.

There is a peacefulness that has settled over this rural area and that wavers only slightly even during the busiest tourist seasons. John and Linda Sisson think that is one of the best reasons to come visit. They bought the inn and opened it in May, 1984. John worked for the Chuck Muer restaurants for several years and Linda was a longtime employee of Leland's well-known Blue Bird Restaurant. Their combined talents produced a blending of competent service and superb food, with a backdrop of beautiful country decor—all of which made the inn an overnight success.

John is unrelenting in his quest to serve "the best." His fish is flown in from the three North American coasts and the linguini is homemade. Every plate that comes out of the kitchen is arranged and garnished as though it was prepared as the subject of an artist's still life. We ate heartily . . . and even in the interest of thorough research, there wasn't room for a single bite of peach pudding, strawberry shortcake, or cherry cobbler.

Although the emphasis here is on the restaurant, like a traditional country inn, there are sleeping rooms available on the second floor. Four are very spacious—large enough to make yourself at home for a few days while you explore the peninsula. The others are small but pretty and comfortable. All are decorated around the country theme,

and when we visited in June there were green plants and freshly cut flowers in many of them.

Overnight guests are treated to croissants, muffins, and fresh fruit in the morning, as well as marvelous waftings from the kitchen while Linda, John, and their skilled staff prepare for another day at the inn.

Vitals

rooms: 10 sleeping rooms that share 4 rest rooms, 2 with showers

children: yes; add $5 per child

pets: ask the innkeeper

smoking: discouraged in sleeping rooms

open season: year-round

rates: $35 through $40

rates include: Continental breakfast

owners/innkeepers:
    John and Linda Sisson
    149 East Harbor Highway (M-22)
    Maple City, MI 49664
    (616) 228-5060

Neahtawanta Inn
Traverse City (Bowers Harbor)

In some ways, Neahtawanta has not changed much from its early days of this century when it was called the Sunrise Inn, or its pre–World War II year as the Ne Ah Ta Wanta Hotel. Sitting high on a bluff overlooking Bowers Harbor, guests came for the area's natural resources, the beaches and clean water, and the beauty of the surrounding woods. There was good food and fellowship, and the kind of deep sleep that comes from days filled with fresh air and activity.

Since the early 1980s, the Neahtawanta Inn has offered friends and casual travelers more than just a piece of the north country. It began as the focal point of a quiet movement, a group of individuals interested in bettering the environment, themselves, and as much of the world around them as they could touch. The goal was to create a place where people could come together to share problems and resolve conflict in close proximity to nature. It was a stopover for restless philosophers of

the 1960s and 1970s hoping to make sense out of the 1980s. We have watched it slowly evolving.

As was the dream of its guiding forces, Neahtawanta hosts individuals seeking rest and retreat, as well as environmental workshops and small groups debating the issues of the day. There is an atmosphere of good health and harmony, reinforced by innkeeper Sally Olson who is a proponent of vegetarian and natural foods, exercise, and late-night discussions around the fire. She gets a helping hand with the daily operations of the inn from her three daughters. "Neahtawanta has an energy all its own," Sally concedes. "I'm just the caretaker of that energy."

For overnight guests, there are four sleeping rooms on the second floor furnished with antique beds and dressers, many of which have been at the inn since its early days. Two of the rooms have lovely original washbasins with marble counters. Recent renovations have produced a bright, spacious third-floor dormer suite available for a family or small group of up to six. The main floor is large and open with plenty of sitting areas, shelves full of books, and a massive sunken fieldstone fireplace.

A Continental breakfast of whole wheat croissants, whole wheat coffee cakes or muffins, juice, coffee, and tea is served family style around the big dining room table. Additional meals may be provided for groups by special arrangement.

Vitals

rooms: 4 that share 1 full bath, 1 suite with private bath

children: yes

pets: up to discretion of innkeeper

smoking: designated area on first floor only

open season: year-round

rates: from $35 single, $45 double, bartering ideas are welcome

rates include: Continental breakfast

owner/innkeepers:

Sally Olson and Bob Russell
1308 Neahtawanta Road
Traverse City, MI 49684
(616) 223-7315

The Old Mill Pond Inn
Northport

David Chrobak's home is reached by a short winding driveway that, in late July, was edged with a profusion of snapdragons, salvia, dahlias, cosmos, and petunias. It gave us the first indication of David's talent with flowers and a hint at the work he has put into plantings throughout the estate. The entire inn was rimmed in perennials. Black-eyed Susans, daises, and lilies were mixed with annuals of all colors. A rose garden bordered a small parking area, and beyond it was yet another garden

enclosed with a fence made of small, unpeeled tree limbs. Flower baskets hung from every porch and encircled a gazebo that David designed and built. By far, the most spectacular of his creations is a huge side garden with four larger than life-size statues of Neptune, Bacchus, Venus, and one of the seasons keeping watch. A Greek column stands in the center.

David has lived on St. Thomas, in the Virgin Islands, since 1969. He operates a flower and gift shop there, but as the island's summer season is slow, he decided to return to his home state and set up a summer residence. He wanted a big house but thought it was senseless to have so much room all to himself. A friend opened a bed-and-breakfast home

in upstate New York, and David was inspired to follow suit. His inn was built as a summer cottage for the Carmen family in 1895. For the first several decades, the interior walls were covered with tar paper nailed to the studs. In 1952, they were finished off with pine paneling. Walking through the parlor and the dining room, you will see that the inn is filled with the handpicked treasures of a well-traveled innkeeper. David's collections of tiny picture frames, crystal and copper, Marilyn Monroe memorabilia, and many other wonderful things adorn the walls and are tucked in numerous glass-fronted cabinets. They fill shelves and are arranged on sideboards, mingling with twentieth-century masters and primitive Peruvian tapestry. David's love of the whimsical is apparent in various pottery pieces and in the appearance of an occasional pink flamingo. During our stay, there were tall jardinieres everywhere, filled with flowers and greenery. It was like walking into a private museum.

Sleeping rooms are on the second and third floors. Feeling that guests seldom use dressers and chests of drawers, David left them out and put comfortable chairs and a sitting area in each room instead. The styles and periods of the furnishings vary throughout the house. Some are more formal, as with the polished dining room set, others casual. The large wraparound porch has several wicker tables and chairs for relaxing and taking in the cool lake breezes. You may be joined by Muffy, David's Westie, or the more shy Molly, a Scottie.

Among his many talents, David is an accomplished cook. Our breakfast began with individual plates of fruit artistically arranged. They were followed by chicken crepes and whole cherry tomatoes sautéed with herbs. On other mornings, David's guests might be treated to eggs with herbs and mushrooms, or a vegetable quiche.

David feels he may be looked on as the town eccentric, a title that makes him smile. He rather likes it. His life is full and exciting, and the Old Mill Pond Inn is a reflection of his joie de vivre.

Vitals

rooms: 5 that share 2 baths

children: extremely well-behaved, over 12 years of age

pets: no

smoking: yes

open season: June 1 through November 1

rates: $50 through $65 per room, roll-away beds $10

rates include: full breakfast

owner/innkeeper:

David Chrobak
202 West 3d Street
Northport, MI 49670
(616) 386-7341

winter address:
23 Store Tvaer Gade
St. Thomas, U.S. Virgin Islands 00802

The Patchwork Parlour Bed'n'Breakfast
Charlevoix

When Mary Ellen Bemus came to the Charlevoix area, she had in mind to purchase a little cottage for herself that could double as an antique shop. After some looking around, she altered her plans a bit and bought a very roomy tourist home built in the late 1880s. There was plenty of room on the first floor for the antique shop, and with the addition of a morning meal for guests, she opened the home for casual bed-and-breakfast lodging. The six second-floor sleeping rooms are reached by an outside entrance off the front porch. Four have small refrigerators and two have a separate sitting area with a table and chairs. Some of the rooms can accommodate a double bed, a single bed, and a roll-away bed, to sleep a total of four. All rooms have a private bath and some have a TV.

Guests are welcome to enjoy the first-floor living room and parlor and to browse in the antique shop. Mary Ellen serves an ample breakfast that includes an assortment of muffins or sweet rolls, juices and fruit, hard-cooked eggs, cheese, and locally smoked whitefish. It is usually available between 8:30 and 10:00, but special arrangements can be made for guests taking the ferry out of Charlevoix. The Patchwork Parlour is just a few doors up from Lake Michigan.

Vitals

rooms: 6 with private baths

children: over 2 years of age

pets: no

smoking: yes

open season: May 1 through October 31

rates: $39 to $49 double occupancy; there is an extra charge for
   additional persons in the same room

rates include: breakfast

owner/innkeeper:
   Mary Ellen Bemus
   109 Petoskey Avenue (US 31 North)
   Charlevoix, MI 49720
   (616) 547-5788

Plum Lane Inn
Northport

Beatrice Bowen opened her country Victorian home as a bed-and-breakfast inn in 1982. From their vantage point, tucked in the wooded hillside that overlooks Grand Traverse Bay, Plum Lane's guests get a lovely slice of Northport life.

"The bed-and-breakfast concept is great for travelers," Bea explained. "Heretofore, we've invited visitors and allowed them to just see. With bed and breakfast, we allow them to get involved and feel—people experience another life-style. Over breakfast coffee, conversation is a stimulating part of the B & B experience."

Bea received a Ph.D. from the University of Michigan, and for the past several years she has been an outspoken and respected educator on the teaching of children's literature. When she retired from her position as a coordinator in the Livonia school system and moved to Northport, her schedule quickly filled with speaking engagements and meetings with special interest groups. But she saved enough time for a

few less intense activities such as the care and feeding of her chickens, organic gardening, and innkeeping. Bea thrives on new experiences.

Plum Lane is beautifully furnished with graceful Victorian accents and reading material that fills a full wall of bookshelves. The three upstairs sleeping rooms are spacious and bright. One has a private screened porch with a treetop view of the bay and an extra sleeping alcove. Guests are invited to join their hostess for an elegant breakfast, most often served in the formal dining room, accompanied by fine china and crystal.

Plum Lane is a great place to unwind for a few days and elude the madness of routine. It is also within easy driving distance of shops, restaurants, and the peninsula's year-round outdoor recreational areas.

Vitals

rooms: 3 that share 1 full bath

children: discouraged

pets: no

smoking: discouraged in the house

open season: spring, summer, and fall

rates: $50 through $60

rates include: Continental breakfast

owner/innkeeper:

    Beatrice Bowen

    Box 74

    Northport, MI 49670

    (616) 386-5774

The Riverside Inn
Leland

The Riverside Inn has undergone many changes since it was first constructed as a boathouse in 1912. Jacob Schwartz, its owner and builder, located it near the original Riverside Inn that he had erected on the banks of the Carp River just after the turn of the century. Schwartz ran a popular establishment, and at the request of his guests he converted the boathouse to a dance hall just a year after its completion. Business was good on the peninsula, and as patrons danced, they must have felt some relief from news of World War I raging on a distant continent.

In 1924, a fire broke out on the third floor of the inn. The efforts of a community bucket brigade helped slow its progress long enough for most of the furnishings to be saved, but the twenty-three-year-old frame building was a total loss. Undaunted, Anna and Blanche Schwartz, Jacob's daughters who had taken over business matters when their par-

ents died, began renovating the dance hall. They had the building turned so it would sit parallel to the river and they raised the roof a half story. By 1925, it opened for business as the second Riverside Inn.

Barbara and Edward Collins bought the structure in 1980, and by then it had gone through several ownership changes. They gave the inn a masterful face-lift with bright country decor and opened a dining room that overlooks the river and serves some of the best food in town. It has become known especially well for its festive weekend cookouts that include New England lobster nights, Bahamian barbeques complete with reggae music and calypso dancing, and fish boils.

Fish boils, for the uninitiated, most often take place around an open wood fire with a large iron cauldron of boiling water suspended above.

Into the cauldron, at precisely timed intervals, are placed potatoes, onions, and whitefish. The Master Boiler then creates a great rush of fire, causing the water to furiously boil over the edge of the pot, taking with it the surface fish oils. The meal is served immediately with cole slaw, breads, and fresh pie. As we write this, many months after our last fish boil feast, we can still remember the cheers from the crowd as baskets of food were brought to the table!

The Riverside's eight upstairs sleeping rooms are individually decorated with country print wallpaper, bed quilts, and antiques. Some have adjoining doors and can be rented as suites. They are all lovely and comfortable.

Both Barbara and Ed are successful artists and gracious innkeepers. They make a practice of hiring local people to work at the inn and they display the works of other local artists. They have contributed much to the community of Leland by restoring the Riverside Inn to its former purpose of good rest and fellowship, and by helping to preserve a fascinating slice of the history of the town.

Vitals

rooms: 8 sleeping rooms, 4 have private baths

children: yes, cribs and cots are available

pets: no

smoking: on first floor only

open season: Memorial Day through Labor Day

rates: $35 through $55 double occupancy

rates include: Continental breakfast

owners/innkeepers:

Barbara and Edward Collins

302 River Street

Leland, MI 49654

(616) 256-9971

Stafford's Bay View Inn
Petoskey

Late in the 1950s, Stafford Smith was working his way through the ranks at an inn on the edge of the Bay View community. The building had been constructed in 1886 on property leased from the Bay View Association and was owned at the time of Stafford's employment by Dr. Roy Heath. It offered fifty-eight second- and third-floor rooms to guests from July 4 through Labor Day.

In the fall of 1960, Dr. Heath actively sought to sell the inn. Stafford, meanwhile, was about to marry Janice, the inn's hostess, and was actively seeking full-time work. The following spring, Stafford approached Dr. Heath about buying the business and they struck an easy deal. Many of the Smiths' early guests were widows or widowers who came up to stay two, three, and even four weeks while attending the Bay View cultural programs. Stafford remembers when vacationers could arrive in Petoskey from Cincinnati by train.

During the past twenty-five years, the inn has undergone several redecorations and rebuildings with each one more elegant and accommodating than the last. Antique and wicker furnishings, bold fabrics,

and richly colored wallpaper give the inn a well-seasoned country look and a feeling of homelike comfort and permanence. Twenty-four second-floor sleeping rooms are used now and may be reached by the main stairway or by an elevator. They face both streetside and bayside, and each is decorated differently with country patterns and antiques. Guests may find such special touches as pincushion baskets with needles and thread, a thick folder filled with information about the inn and the Bay View–Petoskey community, and handmade eyelet and ribbon pillows in their rooms.

The lovely main-floor dining rooms are bright and airy, and Stafford can often be found mingling among the tables greeting friends. The inn's well-deserved reputation for good food reflects years of recipe perfecting and the Smiths' ongoing concern for quality. Many of the selections are reminiscent of what turn-of-the-century guests might have enjoyed, such as steaming bread pudding with raisins and cream. The inn does not serve alcoholic beverages, but houseguests are welcome to bring a bottle of wine to dinner.

Guests are greeted and assisted by a staff that we found to be—without exception—friendly, happy, and very helpful. Among them was manager Judy Honor who has been in innkeeping all her professional life. She formerly worked for both the Grand Hotel and the Harbour Inn, and she keeps things running smoothly.

Stafford's Bay View welcomes children and is well equipped to handle them. On the morning of one of our visits, Janice had purchased another crib to be sure she had enough available for the number of young families that stay at the inn. Stafford explained the perfect setup, "When children get restless at the dinner table, they can climb down from their chairs and play in the common rooms of the inn, which are pretty kid proof, leaving Mom and Dad to enjoy a leisurely meal."

"One of the elements so necessary to the country inn feeling is getting to know the guests," added Stafford. "I love the interplay we have with them. They enjoy being part of historic America, and it's nice to be here and be part of that feeling."

Vitals

rooms: 24 with private baths

children: yes, encouraged

pets: no

smoking: yes

open season: year-round except November 1 through December 25

rates: $65 through $75 single, $80 through $90 double

rates include: full breakfast from the menu

owners/innkeepers:

Stafford and Janice Smith
US 31 North
Petoskey, MI 49770
(616) 347-2771

Walloon Lake Inn
Walloon Lake Village

The emphasis at Walloon Lake Inn has, for several years, been the food, and it appeared, during our brief visit, to be splendid. There are several trout entrées including a fillet of brook trout smoked on the premises; quail stuffed with walnuts and wild rice, served in potato nests with a Madeira sauce; breast of chicken with morel sauce; escalope of pork diablo with roasted chilies, tomatoes, and garlic; strawberry almond duck; a daily veal special; and much more. If there is room for dessert, you can try citrons givrel, daily pastries, homemade ice cream, or any of several other sweet-sounding choices.

In 1986 the five second-floor sleeping rooms were completely renovated and redecorated. They are carpeted and furnished with antiques that nicely complement this nearly one-hundred-year-old structure. Guests share a common area that overlooks the lake.

David Beier is innkeeper, chef, and proprietor of Walloon Lake Inn. If you want to learn some of the secrets of his fine cuisine, ask about his four-day Fonds Du Cuisine cooking school. He offers it periodically during the year; enrollment is limited to six students per class.

Vitals

rooms: 5 sleeping with private baths

children: yes

pets: no

smoking: yes

open season: year-round

rates: $45.00 double occupancy; dinners $12.50 through $18.00

rates include: Continental breakfast (with room)

owner/innkeeper:
David Beier
P.O. Box 85
Walloon Lake Village, MI 49796
(616) 535-2999

Warwickshire Inn
Traverse City

This stately bed-and-breakfast inn sits atop a long hill just outside Traverse City, affording a spectacular view of the bay to the east. The present structure was built in 1902 by the Barney family, but the front of the home rests on a foundation dating from 1854. The lumber used by Mr. Barney to build this country estate came from a wooded parcel that he owned on Long Lake, about five miles away. Barney had the trees cut and floated down the Boardman River to the Brown Lumber Company.

Barney's primary business was insurance, but he also had the first herd of registered cattle in northern Michigan, and he served as president of the Northwestern Michigan Fair for twenty-five years. His house, for the times, was very modern. Gas lights lit the rooms and a second-floor water storage tank supplied the first floor, with an overflow that

ran out to the barn. The home was surrounded by several acres of fruit trees, earning it the name Orchard Lawn. Much of the nearby land still belongs to the Barney family, and the road retains the family name.

Pat and Dan Warwick bought the homestead in 1976 after Dan retired from a career with the Air Force. They finished raising five children and opened their home as a bed-and-breakfast lodging in October, 1983. The furnishings at Warwickshire are a sophisticated and comfortable blend of the old country and the new. Some of the fine antiques, including an elegant hand-crocheted cover on one of the beds, originally belonged to Dan's grandmother. There are also pieces that the Warwicks brought back from their residences in Germany and England while with the Air Force. They complement handsome old wardrobes, rockers, and dressers with rich patinas and their own interesting histories. The warm country feeling is enhanced by the scent of cinnamon and spices that Pat often simmers in a pot on the stove.

Breakfast is elaborate and elegant, served on Wedgewood china with fine silver service. There again, you will be treated to pleasantries

that the Warwicks brought back from their world travels such as coddled eggs and marmalades.

The peacefulness of rural life at Warwickshire belies its actual closeness to Traverse City and all the conveniences of downtown. Sugar Loaf is also just a short drive away, as are beaches and antique shops, cross-country skiing trails, and Interlochen Arts Academy.

Vitals

rooms: 3 rooms, 1 on the first floor with a private bath, the second-floor rooms share 1 bath

children: over 10 years of age

pets: no, but there is a kennel nearby

smoking: yes, in designated areas

open season: year-round

rates: $55 through $60 double occupancy

rates include: breakfast

owners/innkeepers:
Pat and Dan Warwick
5037 Barney Road
Traverse City, MI 49684
(616) 946-7176

Windermere Inn
Beulah

The Windermere Inn was built about 1895 and served as the homestead for a large working farm that wrapped around the northeast corner of Crystal Lake. It was surrounded by cherry orchards. You can still see the foundations of old outbuildings nearby, and there is an artesian well just out back. As the land passed through ownership changes in this century, most of the acreage was sold off and began sprouting shops and houses. By 1980, the old farmhouse itself was vacant.

Bill and Loralee Ludwig passed by the house for years en route to their own residence on the north shore of Crystal Lake. They always admired the structure but felt it was too big for just the two of them . . . until the day Loralee mentioned that it would make a nice bed-and-breakfast home.

They bought the structure in January, 1983, and spent four months repairing walls and ceilings, installing bathrooms, decorating, and filling it with country treasures. By the time they opened in July, they had brought warmth and sophistication back to the neglected lakeside home.

Guests stay in one of four upstairs sleeping rooms that echo the main floor's casual country style. Each room has a private bath and is accented with lovely curtains and bedcovers that were custom-made by Loralee and her daughter-in-law, Mary. Flowers, candy, and fruit greet each new arrival. The rooms are large enough that you could feel comfortable settling in for a week or so. If you are feeling sociable, you can join the innkeepers and the other guests in the living room or sitting room. Each has a fireplace that the Ludwigs keep fed on cold nights. Continental breakfast is served amid linen, silver, crystal, and fine china in the handsome dining room.

The Windermere Inn is a great place to hole up for a while with Crystal Lake just across the street and the quaint little villages of Beulah

and Benzonia nearby to explore. But, it is also a good destination point from which to branch out during the day and return each evening. Within an easy drive are sandy Lake Michigan beaches, the Sleeping Bear National Lakeshore, Interlochen, numerous golf courses, small inland lakes with good fishing, and outstanding winter skiing.

Vitals

rooms: 4 with private baths

children: no

pets: no

smoking: yes

open season: year-round

rates: $60 per room that will accommodate two adults

rates include: Continental breakfast

owners/innkeepers:
  Bill and Loralee Ludwig
  747 Crystal Drive
  Beulah, MI 49617
  (616) 882-7264

Wood How Lodge
Northport

Wood How Lodge is located near the tip of the Leelanau Peninsula, set a couple hundred yards off the road in a clearing in the forest. When you have had enough of noise and crowds, come to Wood How and experience the same stillness that attracted its first owner nearly seventy years ago.

Francis Henry Haserot was a wealthy businessman, and one of his more successful endeavors was cherry farming on the Leelanau Peninsula. He built Wood How as a summer home near what was once the largest cherry orchard in the world.

Haserot employed local Indians to design and construct the lodge. For much of the building material, they felled ancient trees in the surrounding forest. Some of the pine logs used for the lodge walls measure forty-five feet long and more than a foot wide. Many of the floors are maple. To make the fireplaces, the Indians individually se-

lected and split stones, and then matched the halves so that one side of the stonework is nearly a mirror image of the other. The integrity of the structure and the quality of the work attest to the fine skills of the Indian craftsmen.

In the spring of 1928, Herbert Hoover was president and Michigan's Governor Green offered him the use of Wood How as a summer White House. Hoover, unwisely, chose instead to go to California.

Kay and Charly Peak bought the estate in 1978 and live in one section of the lodge. They offer five sleeping rooms, many with king-sized beds; guests share a huge first-floor living room with comfortable furniture grouped around the fireplace. Breakfast is served in the built-in enclosed porch. Across the sunny commons are a stone facade carriage house and stable that Kay and Charly converted to two large cottages. One has three bedrooms and two baths. The other has two bedrooms and one bath. Both have complete cooking facilities and a wood-burning fireplace. They may be rented for extended stays and are ideal for small groups or families.

In spite of its massiveness, Wood How feels cozy and peaceful. It is quiet except for the sounds of the wind and the wildlife, and on clear nights the stars are incredibly bright. The Peaks emphasize that Wood How is very casual, which is part of what makes it such an inviting retreat. It is a great place to settle back for a few days.

If you are looking for more activity, you will find public facilities for hiking, bicycling, fishing, swimming, and boating all within a few minutes drive. The picturesque old Northport Lighthouse is two miles to the north, and Woolsey Airport (affectionately known as Northport International) is two miles to the south. Pilots and passengers who stay at Wood How can rely on Kay or Charly to provide shuttle service to and from the airport.

Vitals

rooms: 5 in the lodge that share 2 full baths, also a 2-bedroom cottage and a 3-bedroom cottage

children: no

pets: no

smoking: common rooms only

open season: mushroom season through color season

rates: $55 through $65 double occupancy in the lodge, $375 to $400 per week for cottages

rates include: Continental breakfast for lodge guests

owners/innkeepers:
Kay and Charly Peak
Route 1, Box 44E
Northport, MI 49670
(616) 386-7194

Gordon Beach Inn, *Union Pier*
Hidden Pond Farm, *Fennville*
The Inn at Union Pier, *Union Pier*
Kemah Guest House, *Saugatuck*
The Kirby House, *Saugatuck*
The Last Resort, *South Haven*
Morning Glory Inn, *Montague*
The Park House, *Saugatuck*
The Parsonage 1915, *Holland*
Pebble House, *Lakeside*
Pentwater Inn, *Pentwater*
Rosemont Inn, *Douglas*
Singapore Country Inn, *Saugatuck*
The Stagecoach Stop, *Lamont*
Stonegate Inn Bed and Breakfast, *Nunica*
Wickwood Inn, *Saugatuck*
The Winchester Inn, *Allegan*
Yesterday's Inn Bed and Breakfast, *Niles*

The Southern Shore

Gordon Beach Inn
Union Pier

Like so many of the old resorts that were open during the 1920s and 1930s, the Gordon Beach Inn has a colorful past. There are rumors of it having served as a gambling joint and a house of prostitution, but by the time Colleen Recor spotted it in 1981, things had quieted down considerably.

It was an orange hotel, all overgrown, with a "For Sale" sign on it, remembers Colleen, and she wanted it immediately. Within three months, she was waist-deep in its renovation. With the help of friends and family, she worked for about a year rewiring, replumbing, and redecorating the old inn.

The original structure had thirty sleeping rooms but Colleen had several of the partition walls removed to make some of the rooms

larger. There are fourteen now, and they vary from small with simple furnishings to large suites with sitting areas, handsome antiques, and private baths. All guests are offered Continental breakfast served in the casual hotel-style dining room.

The focal point of the inn is its expansive lobby with tall windows that let in the morning and late afternoon sun. They provide an elegant backdrop for groupings of comfortable overstuffed couches and a variety of period furnishings. The floors are covered with Oriental rugs. There are books and games for quiet afternoons or rainy days, and on chilly evenings a fire is built in the massive hearth. Colleen can often be found flanked by a pair of longtime friends, her gentle and devoted Dobermans.

Gordon Beach Inn offers four seasons of lodging. A private beach on Lake Michigan, just a short walk away, beckons throughout the year. If you have only thought of the lake as a summer treat, check it out in the spring and fall when the area's changing beauty is enhanced by the presence of migratory wildlife. Winter on the lake can be spectacular. Sometimes the only sounds are the creaking and gnashing of tons of ice shifting indiscernibly on the water.

By prior arrangement, shuttle service to and from the Amtrak station in New Buffalo is available.

Vitals

rooms: 14 with both private and shared baths

children: yes

pets: no

smoking: yes

open season: April 1 through November 1, winter weekends

rates: $35 through $95

rates include: Continental breakfast

owner/innkeeper:

Colleen Recor

16240 Lakeshore Road

Union Pier, MI 49129

(616) 469-3344

Hidden Pond Farm
Fennville

Ed Kennedy was in one of his gardens clipping daylilies when we arrived, and he appeared to be a man totally at peace with his surroundings. He greeted us warmly and gestured toward the flowers. "A friend told me, 'Plant and plan as though you're going to be here forever. You won't be, but someone else will be to enjoy what you've done.'" While showing us his home and recalling how Hidden Pond came to be, Ed mixed prose and poetry, some of his own and some of others, to present the total picture of what he offers guests. And it is this: a lovely home with fine traditional and antique furnishings; twenty-eight surrounding acres of meadow, ravine, and woods; and the opportunity to experience the beauty and peace of life at Hidden Pond Farm.

The first floor of the home is reserved for guests. There are two sleeping rooms, and with them comes use of the living room with a fireplace, a kitchen and dining room, a den, and a breakfast porch. The arrangement is especially nice for two couples traveling together. Ed's own living quarters are in the lower level.

The pace here is relaxed. There are few rules about check-in and checkout. Breakfast is served when guests are ready. Whether visitors choose to hole up in their rooms, take a walk, watch from the deck for deer that visit the pond, or take advantage of the areas's many attractions, Ed hopes they will forget their cares and enjoy the pleasures of this quiet rural estate. He is part romantic, part counselor, part educator, retired from a busy career in the insurance business. He has discovered a deep sense of peace at Hidden Pond Farm and thrives on sharing it. Quoting from the musical *La Cage aux Folles,* Ed reminded us, "The best of times is now."

Vitals

rooms: 2 with private baths

children: no

pets: no

smoking: yes

open season: year-round

rates: $70 per room Sunday through Thursday, $80 per room Friday
    and Saturday

rates include: Continental breakfast

owner/innkeeper:
    Edward X. Kennedy
    P.O. Box 461
    Fennville, MI 49408
    (616) 561-2491

The Inn at Union Pier
Union Pier

It was a bright summer morning when innkeepers Madeleine and Bill Reinke talked with us over breakfast about their experiences creating the Inn at Union Pier. We sat outside at tables covered with white linen and dined on butter-melting popovers, quiche, and bowls of fresh strawberries served with a rum-flavored blend of sweet cream, sour cream, and nutmeg. It was a typical breakfast at the inn.

"When this property came up for sale," remembered Madeleine, "we saw it, fell in love with it, and bought it. Then we sat back and took a real good look to see what we could do with it."

We were entranced with the results.

The first-floor Great Room in the main building serves as a gathering area for all the guests. It is appointed with groupings of furniture upholstered in prints of pink, plum, and forest green that echo colors in the area rugs. Sheer lace panels drape six sets of windows, and during

our visit, cross-breezes from the lake were cooling the room. Chicago jazz spilled from the speakers.

One wall is dominated by a massive Swedish Kakelugn tiled wood-burning stove. It has five interior chimneys that process the smoke and gently heat the room while keeping the exterior tile comfortably warm to the touch. Upstairs in the spacious sleeping rooms, there are five more Kakelugn stoves in different styles. Of the six, two are new and four are quite old, including a round stove built in 1930 that has delicate dandelion designs on the tiles. Also in that sleeping room are two three-quarter beds with a matching dresser from the same period, all original to the inn. They have been refurbished and hand painted with a complementing flower design.

Other sleeping rooms have handsome antique reproduction beds. Each room has a sitting area and full bath. They are air-conditioned and have ceiling fans. The Terrace Suite with its queen-sized cherry sleigh bed and wet bar also has a private balcony. Lovely lace and eyelet curtains are used throughout.

Guests can relax in the outdoor hot tub, and for swimming and beach walking you cannot beat the offerings of Lake Michigan just down the street.

Vitals

rooms: 9 with private baths

children: over 12 years of age

pets: no

smoking: yes

open season: year-round

rates: $65 through $85 double occupancy

rates include: breakfast

owners/innkeepers:
   Bill and Madeleine Reinke
   P.O. Box 222
   9708 Berrien
   Union Pier, MI 49129
   (616) 469-4700

Kemah Guest House
Saugatuck

Kemah is an Indian word that loosely translates as "in the teeth of the wind," and that is where you will find this hilltop home. The oldest part of the structure is believed to have been built in 1906. William J. Springer, an old-world German who sat on the Chicago Board of Trade, bought the estate in 1926 and added unusual Art Deco touches such as a half-circle solarium with leaded glass windows and corner lights, and a tiled fireplace in the living room. Art Deco is often characterized by the predominant use of black and gold with pastel accents. It is very striking but infrequently seen because of the relatively short duration of its

popularity. Springer also commissioned artist Carl Hoerman, a wood-carver, to produce ornate beams, carved panel landscapes, and cornice boards that can be seen throughout the home. He carved Springer's coat of arms in one panel, and in another, this poem:

> In rain and shine
> my port divine
> a world my own
> Kemah my home

There are more surprises. A path that leads to the back of the house will take you to a small cave, complete with stalactites and stalagmites, that Springer built. If you walk along the side property, you will find a stone with poetic verse that marks the grave of an Indian.

Terry and Cindi Tatsch bought Kemah in 1982 and opened for bed-and-breakfast guests in 1984. "We wanted to restore the home with respect to the integrity of its historic architecture," Terry explained. They decorated the large second-floor sleeping rooms with matched late-Victorian furniture sets and beautiful linens that suggest the comfortable life-style Springer must have enjoyed. All the rooms are sizeable. Suite Enchantment, the largest, also has a lovely adjacent sitting

room that makes it a perfect selection if you plan to stay in the area for a few days, or if you are bringing a briefcase of paperwork.

The Continental breakfast is set on silver trays and guests are welcome to eat wherever they want. We chose the bright sun room furnished in wicker with imported Dutch lace curtains and enjoyed the company of other guests staying at this fine hilltop guesthouse.

Vitals

rooms: 4 that share 2 full baths

children: under 12 years of age discouraged

pets: no

smoking: outside only

open season: year-round

rates: $55 through $75 single, $65 through $85 double, 2-night minimum on weekends May through September

owners/innkeepers:

Terry and Cindi Tatsch
633 Pleasant
Saugatuck, MI 49453
(616) 857-2919

The Kirby House
Saugatuck

The Kirby House is a familiar landmark to many in the Saugatuck-Douglas area. It was built just prior to 1890 by Sara Kirby; when she left in 1932, her daughter, who was a nurse, turned the home into a hospital. Over several years it grew from three beds to nineteen and played an important role in the lives of hundreds of area residents until it closed in the late 1950s.

Loren and Marsha Kontio had enjoyed staying in bed-and-breakfast homes throughout Europe and the United States, and they wanted to open their own. By the time they looked at the Kirby House in 1983, it had gone through several ownership and use changes and needed a lot of work. But the Kontios also saw that it had strong pluses—beautiful woodwork, striking architecture, and a site already zoned for commercial use. Their friends rallied around them enthusiastically and offered to help with the renovation. The Kontios purchased it the following

December and began working on it in January. As promised, their friends showed up en masse to help. "Sometimes we had twenty people here on a work weekend," Marsha explained. In all, they estimate that more than forty people helped put the inn together, and the work was completed in just sixteen weekends. They opened in time for the Holland Tulip Festival.

To complement the Victorian architecture, Marsha and Loren selected small print wallpapers and period furnishings, including many oak and brass pieces. The handsome dining room, paneled in the original quarter-sawn oak, becomes an additional sleeping room in the summer. For the added pleasure of their guests, they installed a large outdoor deck, a swimming pool, and a hot tub. A buffet breakfast that

includes fresh fruit and juices, croissants and muffins, and coffees and teas is offered each morning. The Kontios have one house rule, that people make themselves at home and treat Kirby House like their own.

During the school year, Marsha works at Mt. Pleasant High School in the counseling office, and Loren teaches biological illustration and zoology at Central Michigan University. Having summers off has given them a superb opportunity to combine their careers with their love of owning a bed-and-breakfast home. The Kirby House is open weekends in the winter. The four fireplaces are stoked for cozy comfort, and guests may cross-country ski at the nearby golf course. Warm beverages simmering on the wood-burning stove await their return.

Marsha and Loren try to spend some time with each guest, to get to know them and make them feel welcome. They are indeed gracious innkeepers and have brought new life to this fine old home.

Vitals

rooms: 9 in winter, 10 in summer; they share 4 full baths

children: yes, except weekends

pets: ask the innkeeper

smoking: yes

open season: May 1 through December 1, winter weekends

rates: $70 per room weekends, $60 per room weekdays, $10 per extra person in same room

rates include: breakfast buffet

owners/innkeepers: Marsha and Loren Kontio

manager:

David Manke
Center Street at Blue Star Highway
P.O. Box 1174
Saugatuck, MI 49453
(616) 857-2904

The Last Resort
South Haven

Sunsets are magnificent over Lake Michigan, and the large front deck at the Last Resort is a great place from which to observe them and the rest of the goings-on in this busy harbor town. The inn's beautifully painted and trimmed siding, the neat walk and tended grounds give no hint of the condition it was in when Wayne and Mary Babcock bought it less than half a dozen years ago.

Constructed in 1883 by Civil War Captain Barney Dyckman, the building was actually, according to the Babcocks' research, South Haven's first resort. But its spectacular location and once-glorious past could not save it from the fate that struck so many great old summer inns around the middle of this century. By the time Wayne and Mary bought it in 1979, it had been vacant for twenty-five years and was suffering from neglect. They spent three years renovating—installing a

new roof, leveling floors, plastering, painting, and decorating, to produce the gracious lakeside bed-and-breakfast inn you will find today.

Fourteen pretty sleeping rooms occupy two levels of the expansive second floor. Each room is individually decorated with a colorful combination of printed wallpaper, comforters, handloomed rugs, and antiques. Each also has a skirted corner sink with hot and cold water and a handsome wooden shaving cabinet with a mirrored door and plenty of room to unpack toiletries.

Characteristic of many lakeside inns, the rooms are small to medium in size and a few have additional sleeping or sitting areas. Guests have easy access to the beach, just across the street, and to the shops and towns up and down the shore. The Last Resort's breakfast room doubles as a lounge in the afternoons and evenings, and it was the scene of some hot games of euchre when we visited.

Mary is a master at getting strangers to meet across the tables—most often over Continental breakfast. She learns names, occupations, hobbies, and scores of life circumstances about each guest and seems to know instinctively who will enjoy talking to whom. She likens it to working in live theater. Both Mary and Wayne are also artists. Mary's paintings and Wayne's bronze jewelry, as well as serigraphs, hand-painted fabric, ceramics, and photography by other Michigan artists and craftspeople, are for sale at the inn gallery, where guests register.

While still in the grip of "rehab fever," the Babcocks purchased a small guesthouse next door and have renovated it, also. It has two levels, two full baths, and will accommodate six to eight people. Ask for details. And by all means, take a look at the Last Resort's photo album—what Mary refers to as their baby pictures. The "before" shots will give you an even greater appreciation of this lovely lakeside inn.

Vitals

rooms: 14, 8 have connecting doors and may be rented individually or as 2-room suites, all rooms share several common bathrooms with separate facilities for men and women

children: over 9 years of age

pets: no

smoking: there are smoking and nonsmoking areas

open season: early May to September 1; September and October, weekends only

rates: $39 through $59 double occupancy, suites $88, $4 less for single occupancy, reduced rates Sunday through Thursday, weekly rates available

rates include: Continental breakfast

owners/innkeepers:
Wayne and Mary Babcock
86 North Shore Drive
South Haven, MI 49090
(616) 637-8943

Morning Glory Inn
Montague

On the afternoon of our visit to Morning Glory Inn, innkeeper Karen Rouse asked if we might be interested in seeing the fireworks display in Muskegon that night. It sounded like a great idea. A few hours later, she gathered us in her car and headed south, giving us a personal tour of favorite spots along the lakeshore. Karen has many fortes as an innkeeper and we had just discovered one. She is a great resource for information on the area, especially places often missed by the average traveler, and she loves to guide guests in the direction of their interests, whether to old cemeteries, beaches, festivals, the theater, good restaurants, historical spots, or community celebrations.

Karen's home was built in 1881 by a fur trader who was married to an Indian. The yard at one time was filled with large holes where the trader's furs were stored. Although it is over one hundred years old, this house was not the first structure on the property: it replaced a boardinghouse that had burned. An Indian burial ground under the front lawn attests to even earlier use. Karen is the present home's fifth owner, and perhaps because it had always been well cared for and used as a private residence, it was in good shape when she bought it.

Three pretty, antique-furnished sleeping rooms are available for overnight guests. The largest, Suite Dream, is especially nice with its roomy sitting area and lake view. There are plenty of common areas for guests to gather on the first floor, but in good weather the preferred spot is often the fifty-five-foot-long wraparound veranda that catches lake breezes. We enjoyed a delicious and filling Continental breakfast there one bright summer morning.

Ask Karen about her special guest packages that include candlelight beach picnics for two or, in winter, horse-drawn sleigh rides with hot cocoa and snacks. She also plans hockey packages and parlor movie weekends. On the first Saturday of December, guests gather to trim the Christmas tree, have dinner together, and sing carols. Karen says it has been her dream since she was fifteen to be an innkeeper. She takes fine care of her guests and is obviously enjoying a dream come true.

Vitals

rooms: 3 that share 1½ baths

children: no

pets: no

smoking: parlor and outside only

open season: May through Labor Day, Christmas through New Year's, weekends the balance of the year

rates: $35 and $45 double occupancy

rates include: hearty Continental breakfast

owner/innkeeper:
Karen Rouse
8709 Old Channel Trail
Montague, MI 49437
(616) 894-8237

The Park House
Saugatuck

Lumberman Horace D. Moore originally owned much of the land on the east side of the Kalamazoo River in Saugatuck. He operated a shingle mill and a sawmill there, along with two ships to transport the wood to Chicago. He built a large home on Holland Street in 1857, fenced a sizeable, parklike parcel of land around it, and kept a herd of deer to delight his children. The townspeople nicknamed it the Park House—a designation that has lasted 130 years.

Susan B. Anthony came to the Park House at the request of Mrs. Moore, who was concerned about the lack of temperance in the town. Anthony helped found the local chapter of the Women's Christian Temperance Union (WCTU) and was successful in closing six of the town's fourteen saloons during her visit.

By early 1984, the Park House was showing signs of age and neglect. But Joe and Lynda Petty saw its potential. They purchased the

house in January of that year and opened for guests six months later after a whirlwind restoration that included complete cosmetic work plus the addition of central heat, eight bathrooms, a new electrical system, and a new porch. The decor is country, from the brass beds and printed wallpapers to the bowl and pitcher sets, crocks of flowers, ruffled curtains, and rag rugs. The sleeping rooms are small and bright. They have been named after members of the Moore family, and you will find things in each one that reflect the namesake. Mrs. Moore's room has a collection of spools and thread, as though she were about to sit down to her mending. In rooms named for the daughters, you will find a few toys and other children's things. It is quite a nice touch.

Breakfast is served in the big country dining room. It includes a

variety of muffins, granola, fresh fruit, and juice. Lynda said she encourages people to linger at the table and talk. She keeps check-in and checkout times flexible so that guests will not feel rushed. Adjacent to the dining room is a comfortable sitting room with a TV and fireplace that will take the chill out of cool evenings. Fishermen will find the inn's proximity to the Kalamazoo River and Lake Michigan especially convenient. Lynda and Joe have arrangements with several charter boats and will put together special packages that include an early breakfast and a sendoff with a thermos of tea or coffee and a picnic lunch.

Vitals

rooms: 7 rooms with private baths

children: over 12 years of age

pets: no

smoking: yes

open season: year-round

rates: $50 through $65 double occupancy, additional persons are $7 for a child, $15 for an adult

rates include: Continental breakfast

owners/innkeepers:
> Joe and Lynda Petty
> 888 Holland
> Saugatuck, MI 49453
> (616) 857-4535

The Parsonage 1915
Holland

This lovely two-story home is located in one of Holland's quiet residential neighborhoods amid broad lawns and mature trees. It is warmly decorated with many family mementos and antiques. Guests have their choice of four sleeping rooms that share a very spacious bath with a big footed tub. They are also welcome to enjoy the comfortable living room and bright glassed-in porch or the garden patio. A Continental breakfast is served in the dining room to all guests.

The Parsonage 1915 is close to theaters, the business district, and Hope College. Lake Michigan is about a ten-minute drive away.

Vitals

rooms: 4 that share 1 bath

children: no

pets: no

smoking: no

open season: May 1 through October 31

rates: $50 Monday through Thursday, $60 Friday through Sunday, double occupancy

rates include: Continental breakfast

owners/innkeepers:
Bonnie Verwys
Wendy Winslow Westrate
6 East 24th Street
Holland, MI 49423
(616) 396-1316 or (616) 676-0390 between 9:00 A.M. and noon or 5:00–9:00 P.M.

Pebble House
Lakeside

The Pebble House with its jaunty stone facade is instantly recognizable while driving south from tiny Lakeside on Lake Shore Road. It was built as a summer home in 1910 by two couples who were retired from working in the circus. Later, a rapid succession of owners and uses left the estate suffering from neglect. Ed and Jean Lawrence bought the home in August, 1983. It was dilapidated, but had unquestionable character and some surviving attributes. Among them are a late-Victorian-style etched window, a stone fireplace, and wide glassed-in porches. As an artist, Jean approached the project like a giant painting, and the transformation is remarkable.

The main house, with four sleeping rooms and several common rooms, has been completely renovated along with the "little house" and two-story coach house that border the Pebble House tennis court. All the rooms are outfitted with handsome oak and walnut furniture that dates from the turn of the century through the early 1930s. Many of the

pieces are massive, comfortable Mission styles that invite curling up with a book, or settling in for late-night conversations. The Lilac Suite in the coach house will accommodate two couples. The Raspberry Suite in the "little house" has a wood-burning stove and kitchenette and may be rented with the adjoining Blueberry Suite to accommodate six. Guests often end the day sitting by the fireplace talking with others or playing cards together. But several common areas and cozy corners provide ample room for those seeking quiet moments alone. During the summer of 1986, Ed and Jean added a large screen house that is perfect for enjoying the glorious breezes coming off Lake Michigan, just across the street. Nearby, you will find areas for canoeing, hiking, bird-watching, bicycling, and cross-country skiing. The well-known Warren Dunes are only about ten minutes away.

Ed works in Chicago during the week and comes to Lakeside on the weekends. Because he is city oriented, he acts as a catalyst for different directions of conversation. He and Jean have traveled extensively and have fascinating stories of their experiences, not the least of which is their wedding that took place in a seaman's chapel in Malmo, Sweden.

Their love of Scandinavian traditions inspired their selection of breakfast items that include a cold buffet with cheeses, sausages, herring, pastry, and fruit. We loved it! It is served family style around a big dining room table where guests often linger and talk until noon.

The inn is open year-round, subject to the roads being clear in the winter. If you want to reach the area by train, Amtrak stops in New Buffalo and you can make arrangements for Jean and Ed to pick you up. You can also be picked up in Michigan City, Indiana, if you ride the South Shore out of Chicago with Ed.

Vitals

rooms: 4 in the main home, 2 with private baths; suites and single rooms in the coach house and "little house" with both private and shared baths

children: discouraged

pets: no

smoking: discouraged

open season: year-round

rates: $50 through $80 double occupancy

rates include: Scandinavian cold buffet breakfast; 1 suite has kitchenette

owners/innkeepers:
Jean and Ed Lawrence
15197 Lake Shore Road
Lakeside, MI 49116
(616) 469-1416

Pentwater Inn
Pentwater

Pentwater is a busy little resort town, particularly in the summer when vacationers flock to the nearby dunes on Lake Michigan. More than one hundred years ago it bustled with activity because of another natural resource—lumber.

It was during those early logging days that the Pentwater Inn was built as a private residence. In spite of its age, Janet Gunn, who bought the home in 1982 and opened it for bed-and-breakfast lodging, dis-

covered that she was only its sixth owner. Around town, it is still known as the Lewis House after one of its longtime residents.

There are five comfortable upstairs sleeping rooms that are cooled in the summer by fresh Lake Michigan breezes and ceiling fans. When the house was renovated sometime in the 1950s, most of the walls were redressed with knotty-pine paneling, which gives the inn a cozy cottage feeling. Janet encourages her guests to use the living room and dining area for reading or playing games, and on Thursday nights in the summer she is apt to round up everyone to go listen to the band concert in the park. The beach is just five blocks away, and within easy walking distance from the inn are churches, shops, and charter boats.

Fall colors are outstanding around Pentwater, and in winter, you can cross-country ski right out the front door and down the street. But Janet feels what her guests like best about Pentwater is the year-round peace and quiet. "That," she says, "is what keeps them coming back."

Vitals

rooms: 5 sleeping rooms that share 2 full baths

children: discouraged

pets: no

smoking: yes

open season: year-round

rates: $25 single, $40 through $45 double

rates include: full breakfast

owner/innkeeper:
    Janet Gunn
    180 East Lowell, Box 98
    Pentwater, MI 49449
    (616) 869-5909

Rosemont Inn
Douglas

The Rosemont Inn is situated in an old rural neighborhood on a bluff above Lake Michigan, just outside the village of Douglas. The surrounding area is wooded and peaceful and contrasts sharply with the busy resort town of Saugatuck just a few miles away.

The Rosemont's original section was built in 1886 and operated as a tourist home for many years. When Ric and Cathy Gillette bought the rambling structure in 1982, they wanted to update the lodging facilities but retain the warm, casual, country inn atmosphere. They have filled the inn with antiques and Early American reproductions including brass, four-poster, and canopy beds and have added a private bath to each room to enhance comfort and privacy. During the summer of 1984, they built on a wing of sleeping rooms that face Lake Michigan. Each has a gas fireplace, which makes them especially nice in the fall and winter seasons.

True to the country inn spirit, there are common areas in both the old and new sections of Rosemont. The new garden room addition is a skillful combination of contemporary and traditional design. Its cathe-

dral ceiling and plant-laden balcony provide the setting for a two-story view of the heated swimming pool off the back deck. A sandy beach is just across the street for those who prefer lake swimming and beachcombing.

Two wet bars are stocked with soda pop and mixer for guests. If you are a porch sitter, you will enjoy the breezy screened porch and verandas that face the lake. Or you can curl up in one of the big, overstuffed couches in the living room and hide out with a good book.

The inn is well suited for small group gatherings, seminars, and workshops, and the innkeepers welcome inquiries about special arrangements.

Vitals

rooms: 14, each has a private bath, some have a gas fireplace

children: yes

pets: no

smoking: yes

open season: year-round; closed Thanksgiving through Christmas Day

rates: $50 through $75 double occupancy

rates include: Continental breakfast

owners/innkeepers:

Ric and Cathy Gillette
83 Lake Shore Drive
Douglas, MI 49406
(616) 857-2637

Singapore Country Inn
Saugatuck

Denise and Mike Simcik discovered Saugatuck by accident. They used to boat around Wisconsin's Door County Peninsula and decided one year to head inland by river to St. Louis. On the first day of their trip, they were advised of the hazards of river navigation and decided to follow the Lake Michigan shore instead. They came into Saugatuck on a Friday, fully intending to leave in a couple of days, but bad weather held them until the following Tuesday. It gave them time to take a look around the town, and they fell in love with it. Two weeks later, they returned to take a serious look at what was available to develop as a business. Their choice was a small hotel, formerly called Twin Gables, located just across the street from the Kalamazoo River.

According to the tax rolls, Twin Gables was built in 1865 at the river's edge and used as a boardinghouse for employees of the nearby stave mill. When the lumber industry began to decline in the twenties, it

was converted to a hotel. In 1936, the Blue Star highway was built and Twin Gables was moved from the river to its present location. After lean years during the Depression, the hotel made a temporary comeback. Townspeople have told the Simciks that they remember the hotel's excellent cuisine during that time and that it was the scene of many social events. But it closed again in the late fifties and remained so until Denise and Mike purchased it in 1982.

The hotel originally had sixteen small second-floor sleeping rooms that shared two baths. Mike and Denise redesigned the space to produce eight good-sized sleeping rooms, each with a private bath and sitting area, and opened two more sleeping rooms on the first floor. All are decorated differently, and each has a name that aptly describes its furnishings, such as the Jenny Lind Room, the Oriental Room, and the Tartan Room. Denise painted stencils and hand cut wallpaper borders to carry out the individual themes. Her decorating talents are matched by her fluency in languages. In addition to English, Denise speaks French, Maltese, and Italian.

A living room and dining room share the expansive, open first floor and are decorated with country furnishings. Original decorative embos-

sed tin covers the walls and ceiling. Float glass windows across the front give guests a view of the river. Several choices of breads and baked goods, along with fruit and juice, are offered for breakfast each morning. Guests are welcome to eat in the dining room or on the veranda that spans the front of the inn. A large side lawn is available for picnics and summer games.

Vitals

rooms: 10 with private baths

children: over 12 years of age

pets: no

smoking: on first floor, preferred, discouraged in sleeping rooms

open season: year-round

rates: $54 through $80 double occupancy in season

rates include: Continental breakfast

owners/innkeepers:
Denise and Mike Simcik
900 Lake Street
P.O. Box 881
Saugatuck, MI 49453
(616) 857-4346

The Stagecoach Stop
Lamont

The Stagecoach Stop was built in 1859 by Cyrus Dudley and operated for many years as the halfway house between Grand Rapids and Grand Haven. It also, at one time, housed Lamont's first gunsmith shop. Local stories and elements of the home's construction suggest that it may have played a role in sheltering slaves as part of the Underground Railroad.

In 1984, Marcia Ashby and her family opened the home for bed-and-breakfast lodging. Three sleeping rooms are available, including a large suite with a private bath and sitting area. Furnishings are casual with lots of country touches. Continental breakfast is served to all guests.

The village of Lamont is situated along the Grand River and is surrounded by picturesque rolling river valley countryside.

Vitals

rooms: 3, 1 with a private bath

children: yes

pets: ask the innkeeper

smoking: in designated areas

open season: year-round

rates: $50 single, $55 double, additional person $5

rates include: Continental breakfast

owner/innkeeper:
    Marcia Ashby
    0-4819 Leonard Road West
    P.O. Box 18
    Lamont, MI 49430
    (616) 677-3940

Stonegate Inn Bed and Breakfast
Nunica

The Stonegate Inn is located just about midway between Muskegon and Grand Rapids, and for a time in its 125-year history, it was known to travelers as the halfway house along that route. It was also the Ernst family home for 100 years. Present owners are John and Cleo Ludwick. They purchased the inn in May, 1985, from the Zartman family who had opened for bed-and-breakfast lodging the previous summer. The Ludwicks have furnished it with formal Victorian-era antiques and are developing the grounds to also echo the period.

Guests share a common room with a TV and games on the second floor. Continental breakfast is served in the formal dining room or, by request, in a guest's room. This stately brick structure has been beautifully maintained and is visible from I-96.

Vitals

rooms: 3 sleeping rooms, 1 with private bath

children: ask the innkeeper

pets: no

smoking: outside only

open season: year-round

rates: $50 through $65

rates include: Continental breakfast

owners/innkeepers:
John and Cleo Ludwick
10831 Cleveland
Nunica, MI 49448
(616) 837-9267

Wickwood Inn
Saugatuck

If you walk north on Butler Street past Saugatuck's fine shops and galleries, you will come upon the lovely Wickwood Inn. Saugatuck residents Sue and Stub Louis had hoped for years that someone would open an inn in the picturesque village. After a memorable visit to the Duke's Hotel in London, and with two successful Saugatuck businesses already under their belts, they decided to try it themselves.

The solid 1930s apartment house purchased for the purpose was originally built by the family of Frank Wicks, one of Saugatuck's mayors. Prior to that, there was a dwelling on the site belonging to William

Butler, the village's first white settler and the man for whom the main street is named.

Sue wanted to create an inn that would be a wonderful surprise. She wanted it to be the finest escape, but still practical, warm, and above all, comfortable. To carry out the plan, she went to work on the interior with miles of fabrics and wall coverings by Laura Ashley, one of the top designers in the world. Each of the eleven sleeping rooms is decorated around a different theme. The resulting effects are sometimes rich and handsome, sometimes sweet and dreamy, and they are all splendid. Four of the rooms represent the seasons of the year. Another four are suites with sitting areas. The largest suite has a huge four-poster bed and a fireplace flanked by a full wall of honey colored cedar. All of its furnishings are from the Baker Historic Charleston collection.

In each room, guests will find special touches: a hardwood armoire or a marble-topped writing desk, a hand-crocheted canopy, white wicker, fruit baskets, and original paintings. Each also has a private bath stocked with soaps and shampoos by Crabtree and Evelyn.

A cozy, dark, mahogany library bar on the first floor is stocked with setups and good books. Beyond it is the sunken garden room with casual, cushioned wicker furniture and game tables. A set of French doors lead to a screened gazebo that takes advantage of the summer breezes coming off nearby Lake Michigan. During cooler months, guests enjoy gathering by the fireplace in the formal living room.

There is a lot to see here, such as Stub's collection of trains, antique trucks, and cars in the toy room. There are wooden shutters, beautiful rugs, and family heirlooms as well. Everything fits beautifully into the grand scheme.

Wickwood's staff is noticeably accommodating without being obtrusive, and we have always felt well cared for here. We recommend Wickwood to anyone wanting to add to their book of good memories. It is a delightful inn.

Vitals

rooms: 11 with private baths

children: no

pets: no

smoking: yes

open season: year-round

rates: $75 through $110, discounts during nonpeak seasons and to groups renting the entire inn; inquire about business packages

rates include: Continental breakfast, hors d'oeuvres, and setups at teatime

owners/innkeepers:
Sue and Stub Louis
510 Butler Street
Saugatuck, MI 49453
(616) 857-1097

The Winchester Inn
Allegan

The town of Allegan was founded with the development of the lumber industry, and many of its mansions were built by wealthy lumber barons. Alby Rossman came to Allegan as a machinist from New York and set up a forging factory for casting iron. His business prospered, and in the 1860s he built a mansion on what is now Marshall Street.

"At the time this home was built, it was in the country," innkeeper and owner Marge Gavan explained. "Mr. Rossman owned many acres around here. This was his farm. To get to town, he had to take a boat across the river."

As the town grew up around Rossman, he designated a plot of land adjacent to the property as a park. He gave it to the city with the admonishment that if it was not properly cared for, it would revert to the estate. Rossman's mansion and its setting were magnificent in many ways, but one of the most unusual features was the iron fence that still

encircles the grounds. It was cast by a wet sand method called puddling.

Rossman raised his daughters here, and for many decades the house was passed down through the family. For two years during the 1930s, it became a hospital. The birthing room occupied what is now the library. After a series of different ownerships, the Winchester family bought it in the 1940s as their private residence. They loved the home and put a tremendous amount of work and money into preserving it.

Marge Gavan and Gail Miller met when their husbands were stationed with the Air Force in San Angelo, Texas. Both enjoyed architecture, decorating, and entertaining, and they began making plans to go into business together. When they saw the Rossman home, they brainstormed about possible uses and finally settled on making it a bed-and-breakfast inn. They selected a Queen Anne theme that complements the home's Italian Renaissance style, and chose predominant shades of rose and white to provide a rich backdrop for the hardwood floors. The four sleeping rooms are papered in floral prints reminiscent of the period, and each has a sitting area. Small settees and chairs are covered in striped satin and velvet. The manicured lawn and stately trees that

encircle the Winchester blend easily with Rossman's park, which the city continues to maintain. On a warm summer day, the screened porch is a nice place to sit and take it all in.

Beverages and popcorn are available in the evening. A Continental breakfast is served in the dining room. The common rooms on the main floor adapt well for small conferences and retreats, and catered meals for groups can be prearranged. The Gavans and Millers share innkeeping duties. We were fortunate to meet both families and found them enthusiastic and thoroughly enjoying their new venture.

Vitals

rooms: 4 with private baths

children: over 12 years of age, younger children allowed if one party rents all four rooms

pets: no

smoking: discouraged in sleeping rooms

open season: year-round

rates: $45 through $65 single, $55 through $75 double

rates include: Continental breakfast

owners/innkeepers:
Marge and Shawn Gavan
Keith and Gail Miller
524 Marshall Street
Allegan, MI 49010
(616) 673-3621
(616) 673-2379

Yesterday's Inn Bed and Breakfast
Niles

Dawn and Phil Semler's beautiful brick bed-and-breakfast home was built in 1875. They purchased it in 1980 and filled it with lovely antiques as well as furniture, art, and rugs that reflect their travels to England and Korea, where they were stationed for several years when Phil was with the Air Force. Turn-of-the-century antiques mix graciously with brass-detailed Korean chests, oriental glass tables, brass rubbings, and Dawn's own paintings.

Three pretty antique-filled sleeping rooms on the first and second floors are available to overnight guests. The exceptionally large Great Room in the basement is furnished with a king-sized bed, a full-sized sleeper sofa, a kitchen, a TV, and a full bath. It may be rented overnight or on a short-term basis as an apartment. Guests are welcome to share the spacious first-floor living room, patio, and hot tub. An elegant breakfast that usually includes muffins, quiche, potatoes, fruit juice, and a choice of cereal is served in the formal dining room. The menu is varied for guests staying more than one night.

There are many year-round activities that attract people to the area. Dawn says the cross-country skiing is great. Niles gets good, deep snowfalls and there are snowmobile trails maintained in fields leased by the state. Ski World is located in nearby Buchanan. Berrien Springs, fifteen miles away, has a fish ladder that makes salmon fishing popular around the area. I first discovered Yesterday's Inn while on business in South Bend, Indiana, just eight miles south. I can attest to its convenient location and the hospitality of Dawn and Phil. And while I cannot guarantee that there will be hot, homemade peanut butter cookies when you get there (my timing was perfect), I know you will get the kind of personal attention that makes staying in a bed-and-breakfast home so special.

Vitals

rooms: 4 including the Great Room, 2 with private baths, 2 share 1
bath

children: yes, roll-away bed available

pets: no

smoking: not in the house

open season: year-round

rates: $35 single, $40 double, $5 children under 12 in same room
with parents, $10 children over 12 in same room with parents

rates include: full breakfast

owners/innkeepers:

Dawn and Phil Semler
518 North 4th
Niles, MI 49120
(616) 683-6079

Heartland

Blue Lake Lodge, *Mecosta*
Chaffin Farms Bed and Breakfast, *Ithaca*
Clifford Lake Hotel, *Stanton*
Grist Mill Guest House, *Homer*
Hall House Bed and Breakfast, *Kalamazoo*
Hansen's Guest House, *Homer*
McCarthy's Bear Creek Inn, *Marshall*
The Mendon Country Inn, *Mendon*
Mulberry House, *Owosso*
Munro House Bed and Breakfast, *Jonesville*
National House Inn, *Marshall*
Osceola Inn, *Reed City*
River Haven, *White Pigeon*
Rosewood Country Inn, *Adrian*
The Shack Country Inn, *White Cloud*
Stuart Avenue Inn, *Kalamazoo*
Victorian Villa, *Union City*

Blue Lake Lodge
Mecosta

Blue Lake Lodge was built in 1913 on the north shore of Blue Lake just two miles from the town of Mecosta. For the first twenty-six years of its life, it operated as a popular summer hotel—a haven for vacationers trying to escape the city heat. The dining room served good country-style chicken suppers including homemade ice cream for 75¢! It was patronized by local townsfolk as well as the hotel guests.

The hotel closed just before World War II. Nearly forty years later, the structure was purchased and new owners began to remodel. Work was completed by Frank and Elaine Huisgen who bought the lodge in 1976 and reopened the rooms to travelers and vacationers seeking retreat at the quiet waters of Blue Lake.

The fishing at Blue Lake is great. Two other lakes are also accessible, and from the three bodies of water, anglers routinely pull in good-sized bluegill, northern pike, bass, tiger muskie, and sunfish. Guests are invited to bring their own boats and will find plenty of room to tie up.

The lodge's dock has two forty-foot-long sections jutting into the lake with a twenty-foot-long **T**. Rowboats and a paddleboat are also available.

Guest rooms occupy the second floor of the lodge and a section of the first. They are casual and cottagelike, and there are knickknacks everywhere. Towels are stacked in the bathroom for use as needed.

Also on the second floor, for guests, is a large corner common room and kitchenette that looks out on the lake. In addition to comfy couches and a TV, it has a refrigerator, microwave, and hot plate for preparing simple meals. There are gas and charcoal grills outside for cooking the day's catch. Continental breakfast is available each morning, and when the weather is warm, guests will find it set up in the gazebo overlooking the lake.

Blue Lake Lodge is open year-round and is especially peaceful in the winter. By special arrangement, the entire lodge may be rented for small groups. We make one suggestion: The woods are loaded with deer so keep a watchful eye as you drive, particularly at dawn and dusk.

Vitals

rooms: 8 that share 2 full baths and a kitchenette; 9 bedrooms and 3 baths are available to those wishing to rent the whole lodge

children: yes, encouraged

pets: up to discretion of innkeepers

smoking: not in bedrooms

open season: year-round

rates: $30 per room double occupancy

rates include: Continental breakfast

owners/innkeepers:
Frank and Elaine Huisgen
Box 1
9765 Blue Lake Lodge Lane
Mecosta, MI 49332
(616) 972-8391

Chaffin Farms Bed and Breakfast
Ithaca

Sue and Bob Chaffin first began offering overnight accommodations at their home in 1983 during Alma's Highland Festival. The town and its namesake college are just six miles away. Alma is nicknamed Scotland, U.S.A., and this celebration, featuring demonstrations and sanctioned games, is the largest of its kind in North America. The Chaffins so enjoyed their guests that a year later they decided to open their turn-of-the-century home to bed-and-breakfast guests full-time during the summer months. They offer three very pretty sleeping rooms, including a small "children's room" with a single bed and a crib.

"I always admire our ancestors," said Sue of their house design. "They knew what they were doing." Indeed, most of the rooms have windows on three sides to take greatest advantage of cooling breezes, while an orchard was planted to the west to act as a windbreak. On the day of our visit, the temperature was nearing ninety degrees but the house was cool and pleasant. We sat in the big country kitchen and were treated to a basket of hot muffins, samples of the delicious home-baked goods Sue's guests find each morning.

The Chaffins have been farming their land for thirty-three years. Their grown sons, Mark and Mike, have nearby farms of their own now, and together the three families work eighteen hundred acres planted in a rotation of corn, cucumbers, sugar beets, and wheat. "Less than four percent of our population is involved in farming," explained Sue. And with that in mind, she and Bob offer an excellent introduction to farm life. Every visitor is given a farm tour—ours included a ride on a tractor with Bob while he cultivated pickling cucumbers and with their son Mike as he was combining wheat.

The Chaffins are warm, gracious hosts. They offer a wonderful opportunity to see a working farm and help instill a first-hand appreciation for this disappearing way of life.

Vitals

rooms: 3 that share 2 baths

children: welcome

pets: yes

smoking: discouraged inside

open season: May 15 through October 15

rates: $20 single, $25 double, $5 per child

rates include: breakfast

owners/innkeepers:
> Sue and Bob Chaffin
> 3239 West St. Charles Road
> Ithaca, MI 48847
> (517) 463-4081

Clifford Lake Hotel
Stanton

On October 1, 1880, the first telegraph line was stretched from the town of Stanton to Clifford Lake six miles away. Within the next year, a post office was established and the Clifford Lake Hotel was built. A horse-drawn bus line shuttled travelers between Stanton and the hotel for fifty cents a round trip, and vacationers looked forward to riding a thirty-foot steamer that chugged around the lake.

One reporter wrote, "Clifford is becoming one of the most attractive and beautiful places of resort to be found in the state—it will eventually beat the world in progress." Life was easy and pleasures were simple.

Times changed, of course. There were two world wars, a worldwide depression, 3-D movies, and the first person in space. Through it all, the Clifford Lake Hotel endeavored to continue providing services to travelers seeking peace and quiet and good food. But it was beginning to show its age. Norm and Dyanne Eipper bought the nearly

century-old structure in 1976 and began a major renovation to turn Clifford Lake Hotel back into a comfortable lakeside inn. Their success with the project has brought vitality to the whole area, helping to keep a community and a tradition alive.

Half of the first floor of the hotel is a casual country saloon with jukebox music, a pool table, and a lot of local color. The other half is divided into several cozy dining areas that serve real good "mid-western" food. On bright Sunday mornings, diners can sit in the wide glassed-in summer porch and be treated to a bountiful country-style brunch and flooding sunshine.

The sleeping rooms upstairs are stylishly decorated with a mix of antique furniture and collectibles. They exhibit loving touches everywhere—groupings of old photos, a bowl and pitcher, and lace-trimmed pillows. Each room is named after a popular drink such as the Tequila Sunrise Room, which faces east and south and catches the morning rays. There is also a suite, with a living room, bedroom, and full bath, that sleeps four.

What would bring you to Stanton? To begin with, there is the hotel itself—a great destination point with good steaks and seafood, fresh air, and deep slumber. It is a nice place to hole up even in the dead of winter. If you feel like venturing out, you can take your pick of swimming, water-skiing, excellent fishing, an occasional pig roast, various water sports tournaments including car races on the ice and ice golf, boating, nearby hiking, and cross-country skiing. There are three golf courses just a few minutes away and six public tennis courts at nearby Montcalm Community College. Norm and Dy also sponsor a Delta

Queen Night, Summerfest, and a Fourth of July parade. If you take a drive through the rolling countryside, you will see miles and miles of the old stump fences for which Montcalm County has become so well known.

Vitals

rooms: 4 that share 1 full bath, plus 1 suite with private bath

children: not encouraged overnight

pets: no

smoking: yes

open season: year-round

rates: $45 single occupancy, $55 double occupancy

rates include: Continental breakfast

owners/innkeepers:

    Dyanne and Norm Eipper

    561 Clifford Lake Drive

    Stanton, MI 48888

    (517) 831-5151

Grist Mill Guest House
Homer

The Grist Mill Guest House was built in about 1905 for the Cortright family, who owned the large flour mill directly behind it. Its style is described by present owner Judy Krupka as late Victorian, modified Colonial Revival.

Judy and business partner Allene Downing bought the home in April, 1985, from a Massachusetts couple who operated it as a bed-and-breakfast home for four years. When we visited in August, Judy eagerly pointed out many of the features that attracted her to the guesthouse. Among them are fine oak and pine paneling, solid pocket doors, leaded windows, and original light fixtures. Many of the spacious sleeping rooms have canopied beds, purchased from the previous owners, as well as lovely antique dressers and vanities. Most of the handmade, quilted bedcovers were stitched by Judy.

A magnificent restored rosewood square grand piano sits in the living room amid antiques and contemporary art—testimony to Judy's self-described eclectic tastes. Her mix of old and new is attractive and very comfortable.

Weekend breakfasts are lavish and feature such delights as fresh fruit topped with strawberry champagne sorbet or an asparagus–Monterey Jack cheese souffle in a pastry crust with a chicken and romano sauce. A Continental breakfast is served weekdays. Guests staying both Friday and Saturday nights are served a complimentary dinner Friday night. Judy is an excellent cook and continually offers new dishes.

One of Homer's big attractions is the True Grist Dinner Theater

housed in the old mill. It opened ten years ago and offers professional repertoire theater year-round. Most of the Grist Mill Guest House patrons include in their plans an evening at the theater. Judy and Allene will make reservations and secure tickets in advance for their guests.

Grist Mill Guest House is within an easy drive of a great many antique shops, several restored Victorian homes open to the public, seasonal historical walking tours, and year-round recreational areas.

Vitals

rooms: 6 sleeping rooms, 2 with private half bath, 1 with a full bath option, 3 that share 1 bath

children: under 12 discouraged

pets: ask the innkeeper

smoking: yes, except in the dining room

open season: year-round

rates: $40 through $65

rates include: complimentary breakfast

owners/innkeepers:
    Allene Downing and Judy Krupka
    310 East Main
    Homer, MI 49245
    (517) 568-4063

Hall House Bed and Breakfast
Kalamazoo

Hall House sits on a hill adjacent to Kalamazoo College, and one of the unexpected pleasures you may be treated to while staying there is the pealing of the college chapel bells. They ring out regularly in this historic neighborhood of brick streets and well-tended gardens. Henry Vander Horst designed and built Hall House as his private residence in 1923. Vander Horst was a commercial builder in the Kalamazoo area and he has left a number of fine structures, including the State Theatre, as a tribute to his skills. He spared nothing in building Hall House.

Pam and Terry O'Connor purchased the home in mid-October, 1985, and opened for bed-and-breakfast guests the following February. They have been delighted by the home's treasures, which have weathered the decades—among them, intricate moldings and a Dutch landscape on the ceiling of the library, both painted by Vander Horst when the construction business was slow.

The marble foyer with a floor of Detroit-made Pewabic tile is an example of Vander Horst's concern for quality and timeless style.

Throughout the house there is generous use of Honduras mahogany and many built-in closets and drawers . . . some with secret hiding places. An article about the Vander Horst mansion in a 1923 edition of the *Kalamazoo Gazette* (a copy is available at the inn) mentions many of the features.

Pam and Terry named the five sleeping rooms after the home's various owners and decorated each individually, in a variety of styles from contemporary to four-poster elegance. And like Vander Horst, they have paid great attention to detail.

We stayed in the O'Connor Room, originally Vander Horst's studio, which has windows facing west, south, and east. Its striking Scandinavian influence is carried out in the sleek platform bed which we found exceptionally comfortable. This room is well suited for more than two people traveling together or for those wishing to stay for several days. It is very large, with plenty of sitting room and a sofa that opens to a full-sized bed.

Down the hall is the smallest room, named for the Berry family. One wall is draped with a paisley shawl that came from Pam's great-grandmother. To pick up its colors, Pam had the bed, dresser, and

nightstand painted a deep brick red and accented them with forest green linen. It shares a bath with the Borgman Room, which is papered in a rose-colored print to set off the well-polished brass bed.

The Rutherford Room originally belonged to Vander Horst's daughter and has built-in cedar-lined closets and drawers. The O'Connors gave it a bright, informal country look, dressed it in blue and white stripes, and added a weather vane and a beautiful wooden swan. Vander Horst's own room has a queen-sized four-poster bed and a fireplace. The sleeping rooms are reached by an open stairway and a stunning landing with tall windows flanked by two of Pam's brass rubbings.

French doors off the entry lead to the dining room, where a breakfast of fresh fruit and an assortment of muffins and breads is served. The room has a graceful cove ceiling and the formality it lends was complemented during our visit by the quiet strains of classical music and a vase of calla lilies. The ballroom-sized living room has an oak floor and floor-to-ceiling windows that flood the room with morning light. Beyond it is the sun porch, furnished with white wicker.

Terry is a corporate credit manager for Upjohn and also an auctioneer. Ask him for a demonstration! Pam says she feels like a self-appointed ambassador for Kalamazoo, and she knows firsthand the benefits of staying in bed-and-breakfast homes from her experiences in England.

Pam and Terry are proud of Kalamazoo, know the area well, and are eager to assist their guests in enjoying it. Staying at Hall House is a great way to start.

Vitals

rooms: 5, 3 with private baths, 2 share 1 adjoining bath

children: over 12 years of age

pets: no

smoking: in the living room or sun room

open season: year-round

rates: $35 through $56 single, $40 through $61 double

rates include: breakfast

owners/innkeepers:
  Pamela and Terry O'Connor
  106 Thompson Street
  Kalamazoo, MI 49007
  (616) 343-2500

Hansen's Guest House
Homer

Beth and Lloyd Hansen's big Victorian home was built by a Methodist-Episcopal preacher in 1890—an interesting coincidence, since Lloyd is a Methodist minister at a church near Mendon. The home was empty when the Hansens bought it in 1984 and the two have had a great time filling it up. With a backdrop of fine oak woodwork and two marble fireplaces, the overall effect is homey and comfortable.

The Hansens eat breakfast together with their guests. That is a very nice touch and one that most travelers seem to enjoy. It gives everyone a chance to meet and contributes to the "just like one of the family" feeling here. In addition to the True Grist Dinner Theater just a few blocks away, there are many antique shops within easy driving distance, as well as walking tours and golf courses. Canoes may be rented on the nearby Kalamazoo River. If you are looking for gifts, browse through the small parlor shop Beth has at the guesthouse. She keeps it stocked with items from around the globe, particularly Third World countries.

Vitals

rooms: 4 that share 1 full bath

children: ask the innkeeper

pets: no

smoking: no

open season: year-round

rates: $30 single, $39 double

rates include: full breakfast

owners/innkeepers:
   Beth and Lloyd Hansen
   102 West Adams
   Homer, MI 49245
   (517) 568-3001

McCarthy's Bear Creek Inn
Marshall

We met Mike and Beth McCarthy several years ago when they were innkeepers at Marshall's National House Inn. They seemed well suited for the profession. Each has creative interests and artistic skills, personal warmth, and good business sense. They can talk to just about anyone about practically anything, they love Marshall, and they are adept promoters of the town's offerings. It did not surprise us to learn that they purchased their own inn in 1985 and were carrying on the tradition.

McCarthy's Bear Creek Inn is located a mile from downtown Marshall on a high, rolling, wooded parcel of land bordered by its namesake creek. The Williamsburg Cape Cod home was built in the mid-1940s by Robert Maes, a wealthy inventor of farm equipment who also fancied himself a builder of fieldstone fences. You will see his handsome stonework all about the property, connecting barns, follow-

ing the hills, and bordering pastures. The fences ramble amid stately burr oaks and sugar maples, pines and spruces, and the total picture is reminiscent of an English country estate. Mike thinks a flock of sheep grazing in the meadow would be a nice touch.

Seven sleeping rooms in the home have been decorated with a skillful mix of contemporary and antique furnishings. Some of the beautiful bedsteads are family treasures, others are reproductions that blend comfortably with wing-back chairs and watercolor paintings. The original walnut-paneled fireplace in Maes's first-floor library provides a warm, rich backdrop for a queen-sized brass bed. The Garden Room has a private entrance, and two rooms on the second floor each have a balcony from which to survey the farm. Guests staying in rooms that face Bear Creek are treated to the lulling music of water playing over smooth rocks as it makes its way through the countryside.

Breakfast includes a variety of breads and sweet cakes, fruits, cereals, and hard-cooked eggs. It is served in the enclosed porch, where guests can linger with a cup of coffee and yield to the pleasures of life in rural Marshall.

Vitals

rooms: 7 with private baths

children: yes

pets: no

smoking: yes

open season: year-round

rates: $56 through $74 double occupancy, discounts Sunday night
  year-round

rates include: Continental breakfast

owners/innkeepers:

Mike and Beth McCarthy
15230 C Drive North
Marshall, MI 49068
(616) 781-8383

The Mendon Country Inn
Mendon

The Mendon Country Inn has long been a center of activity in this tiny town and has been used for many purposes. The original structure was built in the 1840s to accommodate stagecoach travelers and later, those who passed through the area on trains. It was known as the Western Hotel. In 1873, Adams Wakeman lavishly redesigned the hotel adding eight-foot-tall windows, high ceilings, and a most graceful winding walnut staircase that will catch your attention the moment you walk in the front door.

By 1982 when Lew and Jane Kaiser bought the building, the Wakeman house had been used as a bakery, creamery, and restaurant; as a private residence; and as a place to hold community church meetings. The Kaisers turned it back into a lodging establishment after months of extensive renovation, filling it with antiques and country furnishings.

Each of the eleven sleeping rooms has been decorated around a particular theme. They vary from the cozy, informal Hired Man room to the huge first-floor Adams Wakeman room that has massive arched windows and a creekside porch. Guests will find an abundance of country memorabilia, such whimsical touches as straw hats and Amish dresses on wall pegs, and an assortment of collectibles. Bright, full-sized quilts hang like giant paintings in the second story hall, and the floors

are covered with thick, richly colored rag rugs. A small, first-floor "gathering room" is filled with examples of American Indian art.

Jane's antique shop occupies several rooms on the main floor apart from the guests' common rooms. They are so skillfully arranged that they blend in with the rest of the hotel decor. The shop also provides a constant supply of new furnishings for the sleeping rooms, so do not be surprised if room accessories are different each time you visit.

Breakfast is very casual—usually fruit and juice, coffee or tea, and croissants or sweet cakes. The large dining room can also be reserved for meetings and receptions. From the rooftop garden you will get a panoramic view of the beautiful countryside that surrounds the inn. The area is tranquil and scenic, and rich with Indian history. Canoes for the St. Joseph River, which runs just across the street, and bicycles for local touring are available for guests at no charge. For another look, see the full-color article featuring the Mendon Country Inn in the January, 1986, issue of *Country Living Magazine.*

Vitals

rooms: 11 sleeping rooms, 8 with private baths, 2 that share 1 bath, 1 single with a half bath

children: ask the innkeeper

pets: ask the innkeeper

smoking: yes

open season: May through October

rates: $30 single, $56 through $72 double occupancy

rates include: Continental breakfast

owners/innkeepers:
Jane and Lewis Kaiser
440 West Main Street
Mendon, MI 49072
(616) 496-8132

Mulberry House
Owosso

If you visit Mulberry House in the summer, as we did, you will be greeted by a profusion of flowers and several large gardens that dominate the grounds. They create a beautiful setting for this turn-of-the-century home and provide a constant supply of cut flowers for the rooms. Jack and Carol Holmes bought Mulberry House in 1982 and worked on it for two years to produce the comfortable bed-and-breakfast home you will find today. Guests have their choice of three second-floor sleeping rooms that have been furnished with casual antiques and share one full bath. They are papered with lovely floral prints and bear such pretty country touches as herb wreaths, potpourri hearts, and rose balls. Each has a basket of plush towels and soaps. The largest room has both a double and a single bed and is especially convenient for parents traveling with a child.

A living room on the first floor has been designed primarily for guests' use, as Jack and Carol have their own quarters. Adjacent to the living room is an elegant dining room with a plant-filled bay window and lace curtains through which streams the morning sun.

"I love to set the table with pretty dishes and fresh flowers," Carol explained. She uses crystal and china, and varies the patterns for guests staying more than one night. Breakfast includes fruit and a selection of muffins, breads, or coffee cakes, coffee, and tea.

Guests are welcome to relax on the front porch or the patio. There are many historic sites to be enjoyed in this town, and the curious Curwood Castle, built by author James Curwood, is not far. Carol can also refer you to other bed-and-breakfast homes in the area through the Bed & Breakfast in Mid-Michigan League.

Vitals

rooms: 3 that share 1 bath

children: ask the innkeeper

pets: no

smoking: yes

open season: year-round

rates: $35 through $50 double occupancy

rates include: Continental breakfast

owners/innkeepers:
   Jack and Carol Holmes
   1251 North Shiawassee Street
   Owosso, MI 48867
   (517) 723-4890

Munro House Bed and Breakfast
Jonesville

General George C. Munro built this classic Greek Revival home between 1833 and 1840. Munro operated a gristmill and general store in Jonesville, but according to the county history, he was involved in extensive business both here and abroad. The home passed through Munro's family for several decades until the last of his daughters left it in 1935.

Jerry and Sandy Witt purchased the home in July, 1985, and opened it just three months later. They filled the rooms with furnishings dating from the 1800s. Most are from the Empire period, often characterized by weighty styles, claw feet, and the frequent use of rosewood, tiger and bird's-eye maple, striped satin, and featherstitching. The five sleeping rooms are decorated very individually and some of their names give a clue to the furnishings guests will find. The Shaker Room, for example, is furnished with a reproduction Shaker trundle bed and, in the simple Shaker tradition, has pegs across one wall for hanging clothes. The

ceiling in the Marshall Room has been papered with a rose print and blends beautifully with pale peach carpeting and a handsome brass and bird's-eye maple bed. There are twin cannonball beds in the Stencil Room, and a huge sleigh bed in the first-floor sleeping room named for the original owner. Private sitting areas, rocking chairs, and writing desks abound. Of the home's ten fireplaces, three are in sleeping rooms.

A Continental breakfast is served in a bright dining room, originally Munro's library. It, too, has a fireplace, and a wall of built-in cupboards stocked with mugs, cups, and glasses so that guests can help themselves anytime to coffee and other beverages. Twelve-foot ceilings and interior wooden shutters add to the elegance of the first-floor living room.

Jerry and Sandy are former owners of an antique store in Saugatuck and still dabble in the business. They have done considerable work on this fine home and, with an acute respect for its history, have preserved it for decades to come. If you are looking for activities in the area, they can direct you to the Grosvenor House Museum just across the street and to a nine-hole golf course four blocks down the street. Hillsdale is

five miles away, and just six miles away is the tiny town of Allen with an estimated fifty antique shops.

Vitals

rooms: 5 with private baths

children: four years of age and above

pets: no

smoking: not in the sleeping rooms

open season: year-round except Christmas through New Year's

rates: $53 single, $58 double

rates include: Continental breakfast

owners/innkeepers:
    Jerry and Sandy Witt
    202 Maumee Street
    Jonesville, MI 49250
    (517) 849-9292

National House Inn
Marshall

The National House Inn opened as a stagecoach stop in 1835, two years before Michigan became a state. Like many old buildings, it has gone through several changes of use and ownership through the decades, hitting bottom as a ragged apartment house. In 1976 Norman and Kathryn Kinney and Hal and Jacquelyn Minick purchased the building and began a heroic renovation—the greatness of which can be appreciated only by perusing the before and after scrapbook.

These talented, farsighted owners skillfully recreated a classic

country inn that looks and feels as though it has been serving the needs of travelers continually, with grace and style, since before the turn of the century.

The entry room of the inn has an old plank floor and, at one end, a massive brick hearth where guests often gather. Directly above on the second floor is a large, handsome sitting room with another fireplace. There are sixteen sleeping rooms individually decorated with nineteenth-century Victorian and country-style furnishings. Some of the rooms have gleaming brass beds, while others have hand-carved wooden bedsteads with matching mirrored vanities. The linens and bedcovers are lovely and often echo the periods of decor. Three sleeping rooms occupy the main floor. All sixteen are named for Marshall's early residents, such as the elegant two-room Ketchum Suite, so named in honor of the town's founder. With the inn's choice location on the town circle, many of the rooms have a fine view of the historic Honolulu House or the Brooks Memorial Fountain. There are several common rooms on the first floor and a large country dining room

where a breakfast of fruits and sweet cakes is served. A small gift shop sells great country crafts and antique reproductions.

The innkeepers have had the pleasure of welcoming guests from all over the world and from all backgrounds. Throughout the year they schedule special weekend programs including candlelight tours through some of the city's most famous homes. They also publish a delightful newsletter featuring a schedule of upcoming events at the inn, highlights of past months, and some time-tested recipes.

There is much to see and do at the National House, as well as in this historic town that once thought it would surely be chosen as Michigan's capital. Antique shops abound, and architectural history connoisseurs will find it a paradise.

Vitals

rooms: 16, each has a private bath

children: yes, cribs are available

pets: no

smoking: yes

open season: year-round except Christmas Eve and Christmas Day

rates: $50 through $79 double occupancy, $6 for third person in the same room

rates include: Continental breakfast

innkeepers:
Jack and Sharlene Anderson
102 South Parkview
Marshall, MI 49068
(616) 781-7374

Osceola Inn
Reed City

The Osceola Inn has been the center of activity in Reed City for the better part of a century. It was built as the King Hotel back in the 1890s and flourished in this town lucky enough to have the train tracks crossing in all four directions. Tom Eichenberg has worked at the hotel for the last thirty years—since he was thirteen years old. He owns it now, along with partner Ed Rogala, who also works at Ferris State College.

Tom was born in Reed City and feels a sense of responsibility to the community, but in addition, he is capable and innovative. The decisions he made in the past couple of decades affecting the hotel have been good ones and account for its continuing vitality and importance in the town.

The most popular aspect of the Osceola Inn is its restaurants that serve everything from light "California-style" entrées to old-fashioned home cooking. On Friday and Saturday, Tom puts on a smorgasbord with fifty different salads, fourteen entrées, and a dozen desserts.

The fourteen second-floor sleeping rooms have been redecorated and have private baths, cable TV, and air-conditioning. Third-floor rooms have shared bathrooms. The hotel is not fancy and makes no claims for romantic ambiance, but it does offer inexpensive, comfortable lodging, good food, and a taste of friendly small-town hotel activity. The North Star bus line stops there. Desk clerks are on duty twenty-four hours and telegraph service is available. There is a barber shop—would a hotel be complete without one?—and if you are passing through the town but do not have time for a full meal, you can stop at the bakery and delicatessen and take a little bit of the Osceola Inn with you.

Vitals

rooms: 27 sleeping rooms and suites, 14 have private baths

children: yes

pets: yes

smoking: yes

open season: year-round

rates: rooms $15 through $45, suites $34 through $45

rates include: morning coffee

owners/innkeepers:

    Tom Eichenberg and Ed Rogala
    110 East Upton Avenue
    Reed City, MI 49677
    (616) 832-5537

River Haven
White Pigeon

Jim and Blanche Pressler live in a lovely brick ranch-style home on a bank above the St. Joseph River and are part of Patchwork Quilt Bed and Breakfast based in Middlebury, Indiana. Situated just a few miles north of the Michigan-Indiana state line, their home is surrounded by lush orderly farms and is close to Amish communities, flea markets, and the renowned Shipshewana auctions. They call it River Haven.

In keeping with the flavor of the area, this bed-and-breakfast home is filled with country furnishings, crafts, and family memorabilia. The beds in each of the three guest rooms are covered with custom Amish-made quilts and pillows in traditional patterns. Our room was decorated in blues and accented by a quilt that was pieced in shades of an early morning summer sky. Some of the rugs and furnishings have been made by the Presslers' Amish friends and may be purchased or custom ordered. Jim urged us to try out a pair of Amish-made rocking chairs

that were new since our first visit. They were fashioned of slats and branches, with the branches used like bentwood, and were remarkably comfortable.

Jim, it seems, can do *anything* well, but his skills are most immediately obvious in the large gardens all around the home. He grows a variety of flowers, fruits, and vegetables in the rich river valley soil, and his love for the river is apparent. Sometimes he and Blanche get up very early in the morning and sit on their back porch just to listen to the rest of the world waking up. Jim explained, "We come out here and listen to the fish flopping and the birds starting to sing and the rooster crowing on the other bank. The river is full of life at that time."

Blanche is an accomplished cook and baker. Her delicious rolls

and breads are offered to River Haven guests in the morning when they gather around the big dining room table to enjoy a hearty breakfast. Blanche also provides lots of little "extras" such as the lemonade and cookies we received on arrival.

River Haven is a warm, relaxed, quietly Christian home. The Presslers are kind, gentle people with a gift for easy conversation and a genuine ability to make their guests feel welcome.

Vitals

rooms: 3 sleeping rooms, 1 with a private bath, 2 share a full bath and a half bath

children: yes

pets: no

smoking: not in the house, but guests are welcome to join Jim outside

open season: year-round

rates: $35 single, $45 double, $10 each extra person

rates include: full breakfast

owners/innkeepers:
Blanche and Jim Pressler
9222 St. Joe River Road
White Pigeon, MI 49099
(616) 483-9104

Rosewood Country Inn
Adrian

You will find the Rosewood Country Inn at the end of a long driveway that meanders through old stands of pine and hardwoods. The original portion of the structure was built during the late 1800s, and at the turn of the century it was part of a 160-acre working farm with a thriving dairy business. In 1950, Dr. Howard Heffron purchased the farm and remodeled the home extensively, adding three wings and supplying the Williamsburg influence that is still evident today. He was also responsible for extensive plantings, including many fruit trees, that give the grounds a parklike quality. Innkeepers Pat and Don Rose took us for a walk around the estate and pointed out some of the unusual trees, such as the sweet gum, that Heffron cultivated.

The Roses bought this marvelous country home, with ten acres, in April, 1985, and opened for bed-and-breakfast guests the following September. They used colonial-style furnishings, including wing-back

chairs and braided rugs on hardwood floors, to play up the traditional lines of the home. There are touches of country-folk decor but always used sparingly to enhance the clean, uncluttered look. The sleeping rooms are large and bright, furnished with antiques and decorated with a predominance of blues and white. The total effect is simple country elegance. We had not seen it so well done before and were quite taken with it.

A Continental breakfast of muffins or rolls, fruits and juice, and specialty coffees is served during the week at the guests' convenience to accommodate those who have to make early-morning meetings or business appointments. On the weekends, breakfast is set up in the dining room, just off the expansive living room.

Pat and Don both attended nearby Adrian College. Don is an ele-

mentary school principal and Pat is a former teacher. They are a delightful couple and, along with their children, Julie and Brian, spread much
warmth throughout this inn.

Vitals

rooms: 4, 2 with private baths

children: ask the innkeepers

pets: no

smoking: yes, except in sleeping rooms

open season: year-round

rates: $36 through $42 double occupancy

rates include: Continental breakfast

owners/innkeepers:
>   Don and Pat Rose
>   3325 South Adrian Highway (M-52)
>   Adrian, MI 49221
>   (517) 263-5085

The Shack Country Inn
White Cloud

Janette and Marv Deur were both born and raised within ten miles of the Shack but knew little about it before they bought it in 1976. The name of this inn is misleading. It is actually a very large and well-built log lodge constructed in 1945 from trees that grew in a stand seven miles east of the property. It sits on 75 acres of meadow and woods and overlooks 120-acre Robinson Lake. This is the second log structure to occupy the land. The first was built in the early 1900s but it burned down in 1942. It was called the Shack, and the name has stuck. The present lodge was constructed by a furniture dealer from Grand Rapids, who, apparently not wanting this log structure to suffer the same fate as the first, added built-in fire hoses and a water-pumping system.

The lodge has a huge first-floor living room with groupings of comfortable couches and chairs, a built-in TV, a pool table, and a fireplace. A bow window spans one end of the room, affording a great view of the lake. A few years ago the Deurs added an adjacent dining room with a matching bow window. It is there that guests most often eat

breakfast—a big country breakfast of eggs, bacon or sausage, toast, cereal, juice, and coffee. The menu is varied for guests staying more than one night and will sometimes include pancakes or French toast with maple syrup from the Deurs' own sugarbush. Evening treats usually include ice cream and sometimes Janette's home-baked desserts. Additional meals for groups may be arranged.

In keeping with the scale of things in the lodge, the sleeping rooms are also big. Three are furnished with two double beds and three have a combination of double and twin beds, accommodating a total of about twenty-four guests. Paintings and prints, antiques, oil lamps, collections of dishes and knickknacks are found throughout the lodge—many against the backdrop of smooth, lacquered logs that lend a warm, homey feeling. And always there is the unmistakably delicious scent of wood mingling with whatever good things Janette is baking in the kitchen.

There is a sandy beach just in front of the lodge, and Marv says the fishing in Robinson Lake is above average. Anglers routinely pull in large- and smallmouth bass, pike, bluegill, and perch. Many are also successful at spear fishing. Guests have the use of a fishing boat, canoe, and paddleboats at no extra charge. Lodge guests are often members of

a wedding party or those gathering for family or class reunions. "This is a good place for quiet adult relaxation," Marv explained.

There is plenty of room to picnic and play games on the lawn. Within easy driving distance are two golf courses. If you plan a spring visit, you may want to time your stay to coincide with the sugarbush. Janette and Marv, with the help of their children, produce about seventy gallons of syrup during a good season, and you will be welcome to help carry the sap buckets. It is an exhilarating springtime tradition and a lot of fun.

Vitals

rooms: 6, 3 have private baths with showers, 3 have private lavatories with a stool and sink and 1 shared shower

children: by special arrangement

pets: no

smoking: yes

open season: year-round

rates: $30.00 single, $40.00 and $45.00 for a couple in 1 bed, $42.00 for a couple in 2 beds, $7.50 per additional person in the same room

rates include: breakfast

owners/innkeepers:
Marv and Janette Deur
2263 West 14th Street
White Cloud, MI 49349
(616) 924-6683

Stuart Avenue Inn
Kalamazoo

There was a lot of money in Kalamazoo at the turn of the century, and the city has several blocks of mansions in various states of repair to prove it. One of the area's first wealthy residents was U.S. Senator Charles Stuart, who built an Italianate villa on the outskirts of the business district in 1854. Few others moved in around him because only the wealthiest could afford a private horse and buggy to ride to work in town each day. In the 1880s, horse-drawn trolleys were put on the streets making the exclusive neighborhood more accessible. By the 1890s, the Stuart neighborhood was filled with magnificent architecture representing various periods.

One of the homes was a large Queen Anne residence on Stuart Avenue built by Frank Cowgill in 1889. It was described in a history of Kalamazoo as having achieved a timeless serenity.

Young James Balch came to the progressive river town of Kalamazoo to attend Kalamazoo College. He married, became a successful

businessman, and eventually served three terms as mayor of Kalamazoo during World War I. Balch and his wife, Mabel, bought the Queen Anne home from Frank Cowgill's widow and lived there for half a century.

By the time Bill and Andy Casteel bought the home in July, 1983, it had been divided into apartments. They spent a lot of time "undoing," and then began restoring the building with the kind of determined spirit that is spreading through the historic neighborhood. They opened their doors as a bed-and-breakfast home three months later.

There are six sleeping rooms available to guests. All are beautifully decorated and furnished in the style of the late 1800s with bold, Victorian reproduction wallpaper and fine antiques. Most of the bedsteads are handsome reproductions in queen size. Two of the rooms have fireplaces and one also has a small kitchen and private entrance. Each room has a private bath, cable TV, and a telephone.

The Eastlake sitting room on the second floor is open to all guests. It is a wonderful place to sit and read or gather with others to share a

bottle of wine before dinner. Croissants and sweet cakes are served for breakfast in the main-floor dining room—one of the cheeriest we have seen. The morning light streams in through ten windows. Stroll around the grounds of the home and you will see some of the work that Andy and Bill put into re-creating a turn-of-the-century look outside. You will also find their traditional rose garden in bloom throughout the summer.

Bill retired from Kalamazoo's Upjohn Company and is a partner in the West Hills Athletic Club. If you are up early enough, you may be able to join him for a run around the Stuart neighborhood. He and Andy are both delightful company.

We recommend Stuart Avenue especially to business travelers and to those for whom bed-and-breakfast lodging is a new experience. If you are planning an extended stay in the Kalamazoo area, ask about the other homes that Bill and Andy have renovated in the historic Stuart neighborhood. They are available for short-term rental and offer surroundings similar to the inn.

Vitals

rooms: 6, all with private baths; Melinda's Room also has a small kitchen and a separate entrance

children: over 12 years of age

pets: no

smoking: not permitted in the house

open season: year-round

rates: $45 or $50 for a single, double occupancy $5 additional, weekly rates available

rates include: Continental breakfast

owners/innkeepers:

Bill and Andy Casteel
405 Stuart Avenue
Kalamazoo, MI 49007
(616) 342-0230

Victorian Villa
Union City

The Victorian Villa is as much a living lesson in Victorian history and culture as it is a romantic bed-and-breakfast inn. This magnificent structure was commissioned to be built in 1872 by Dr. William P. Hurd and completed four years later at a cost of twelve thousand dollars. Craftsmen who erected the ornate home worked for as little as eight cents a day.

Dr. Hurd had come to Union City from Genesee County, New York, several years earlier to join his brothers in a medical practice. He also became founder and chairman of the National Bank of Union City. But in 1881, after living in his Victorian mansion for only five years, Dr. Hurd died of a kidney ailment. Caroline Hobart Hurd, whom the doctor

had wed in 1842, continued to live in the home until her death in 1910. In 1950, the mansion was converted to apartments.

Ron Gibson first discovered the Victorian Villa in the early 1970s, but he had to wait for seven years—persistent, eager, and full of grand plans—until the owner would sell it. His first task, assisted by his wife Sue, was to undo several decades of "modernization." You will find the home now, like a tiny museum, filled with the lace and finery, crystal, oil paintings, parlor plants, printed wallpaper, and furniture that exemplify various periods of the Victorian era. Everywhere you look, you will see the quality of workmanship that was built into the remarkable home more than one hundred years ago.

The eight bedchambers are each distinctively decorated in a popu-

lar style of the 1800s and named for the periods they represent. They begin with 1840s Empire and continue with Rococo, Renaissance, Eastlake, and Edwardian. The second-floor Victorian Country Suite has a viewing balcony overlooking the estate gardens. On the third floor are two Victorian Tower suites that share an adjoining parlor.

Although there are antique shops and great pastoral scenes within an easy drive of Victorian Villa, we classify this jewel as a destination inn—a place where you can go to imbibe the gentle side of life. Ron has observed, "People often come here to get away from everything else. They come to celebrate special occasions. For some it's a time just to get reacquainted, a time to fall in love again."

Accommodations at Victorian Villa include an afternoon beverage that varies depending on the season, and an extended Continental breakfast. At a guest's request, Ron can make arrangements for champagne or wine, hors d'oeuvres, and flowers. Ask, also, about the sumptuous twelve-item Victorian tea that will be served by reservation in the afternoon or early evening. It has a varying menu that includes madeleines, Battenburg cakes, crumpets, and scones with jams made from the fruits in the Victorian-styled gardens that surround the inn. Special old-fashioned Victorian weekends are planned throughout the year. Victorian Christmas weekends held between Thanksgiving and New Year's will give you the opportunity to partake in the roast goose and plum pudding, magic shows, caroling, and wassail of an old-fashioned holiday. New to the repertoire are Sherlock Holmes Mystery weekends and Summer Daze weekends, complete with candlelight croquet and ice-cream churning.

Vitals

rooms: 8 sleeping rooms, 6 have private baths, 2 share 1 bath

children: no

pets: no

smoking: not permitted inside

open season: February through December

rates: $55 through $70 double occupancy

rates include: Continental breakfast and afternoon beverage

owners/innkeepers:
   Ron and Sue Gibson
   601 North Broadway
   Union City, MI 49094
   (517) 741-7383

Metro

The Botsford Inn, *Farmington Hills*
The Garfield Inn, *Port Austin*
Governor's Inn, *Lexington*
The Homestead, *Saline*
Lake Street Manor, *Port Austin*
Mayflower Hotel, *Plymouth*
Montague Inn, *Saginaw*
Murphy Inn, *St. Clair*
Oakbrook Inn, *Davison*
Raymond House Inn, *Port Sanilac*
Vickie Van's Bed and Breakfast, *Lexington*
The Victorian Inn, *Port Huron*

The Botsford Inn
Farmington Hills

"This was Henry Ford's own furniture," John Anhut said as we stood in an alcove of the living room at the Botsford Inn. He ran his hand gently over the back of a tall rocker and across the polished surface of a round wooden table. John's reverence for Ford is obvious. And after thirty years as owner and keeper of the inn that for a time belonged to the benevolent millionaire, he still seems awed by it all.

There are different versions of what led to Henry Ford's purchasing the inn. The most frequently told is that he was courting his wife-to-be, Clara, the first time he saw it. Out of that nostalgia, Ford bought the place and restored it.

That was in the early 1920s and the building and business were already eighty years old. The original structure had been built by Orrin Weston in 1836 to be a private home. Five years later, Stephen Jennings

THE BOTSFORD INN

This historic inn, the oldest in Michigan still providing food and lodging, was built as a home in 1836 by Orrin Weston. In 1841 it was converted into a tavern by Stephen Jennings. Known as the Sixteen Mile House, it was the stagecoach stop here in Clarenceville on the Grand River plank road, which followed an Indian trail that went on to Lake Michigan. Milton C. Botsford in 1860 acquired the inn. It became a popular meeting place for drovers, farmers, and travelers to and from Detroit. Henry Ford, who had first seen the inn while courting his future wife, Clara, in a horse and buggy, purchased the inn from the Botsfords in 1924 and restored it. The Fords operated it until 1951.

bought it and turned it into a general store and very popular tavern called the 16 Mile House. Located on what was then the Grand River Trail, it served as a convenient stop along the Lansing-Detroit stage-coach route.

In 1860, it was sold again, this time to Milton Botsford who gave the inn his name. The Botsfords held frequent dances in the ballroom and, on one fortuitous evening, young Henry Ford and Clara Bryant attended. Ford bought the inn in 1924 and started pouring money into it . . . hundred of thousands of dollars over a period of just a few years. He also moved it back from the main road about three hundred feet and put new footings under it.

John Anhut purchased the inn from Ford's estate in 1951. Since that

time, three additions have been built that are so skillfully designed and furnished it is difficult to tell where the old stops and the new begins.

The theme is Early American from the wooden bedsteads and wing-back chairs in the sleeping rooms to the turkey and dressing and chicken pies on the dinner menu. The heavy, supporting ceiling beams and smooth, old wooden floors will take you back to the time when Detroit was a full day's carriage ride from the inn. You will also see fine furnishings throughout that were collected from around the world and placed in the Botsford by Henry and Clara years ago. Stroll through the main floor and you will find the original dining room paneled with corncob-smoked soft pine, and the 150-year-old original kitchen that served the needs of hungry travelers for so many decades. It is easy to imagine a tired horseman pulling off his dusty boots and ordering a mug of beer . . . a coach rolling up to unload its weary passengers and gather fresh horses. The feeling is warm and inviting, and the sense of tradition is strong.

Vitals

rooms: 68 rooms, all with private baths

children: yes

pets: no

smoking: yes

open season: year-round

rates: $50 and $60 single, $55 and $65 double, $65 through $125 suites

rates include: room only

owner/innkeeper:
    John Anhut
    28000 Grand River
    Farmington Hills, MI 48024
    (313) 474-4800

The Garfield Inn
Port Austin

We began our visit to the Garfield Inn by feasting on a hearty buffet breakfast one sunny Sunday morning in June. The buffet is a Sunday tradition at the inn. Our choices included platters of fresh fruit, juices, potatoes, breakfast meats, scrambled eggs, coffee cakes, and French toast with maple syrup. It was ample and delicious. Afterward, owners Gail and Gary Regnier took us on a tour and told us the history of this beautiful structure.

Records date the construction of the earliest section of the inn at around 1820, but most of the building took place in the 1850s. Charles and Maria Learned purchased it in 1857. Charles was a very successful contractor who worked on big projects like the Erie Canal, the New

York and Boston waterworks systems, and railroads. By the 1850s he had moved into farming and lumber. It was during a search for good pine that he came to Port Austin. Having been raised in New York State, Charles became enthralled with Michigan's wild beauty and the economic potential of its woods. He purchased nine thousand acres of timberland near Port Austin and moved his family to the big towered house in town.

Among the Learneds' friends was James A. Garfield. They had met in Poestenkill, New York, when Garfield, at the age of twenty-six, took a position as preacher there. By the mid-1860s, Garfield was serving as a U.S. Congressman in Ohio. In October, 1866, he visited Maria and Charles in Port Austin, stayed at their home, and delivered a stirring two-hour speech at the courthouse. Three years later he returned and, from the balcony of the Learned home, spoke to the town on behalf of the presidential bid of Ulysses S. Grant. In letters and diaries Maria and James confessed a deep love for each other, brought about, in part, through their sharing of strong religious convictions. Maria died in January, 1881, of tuberculosis, and a few months later Garfield, then president of the United States, was assassinated.

With an understanding and appreciation for the historical value of this building, the Regniers purchased it in the fall of 1982 and began renovating and preserving it. The home had been used for several years as a hotel and bar, and then it sat empty. Gail and Gary secured a new liquor license and submitted an application to have the home declared a National Historical Site. After installing more than eight hundred sheets of drywall, they redecorated with deep, rich wall and carpet colors and furnished it with a combination of antiques and special collection reproductions. Oriental rugs are used throughout the first-floor dining rooms. In addition to the Sunday buffet, the restaurant and bar offer lunch and dinner with a menu that includes a good selection of sandwiches, several fish entrées, and steaks. You can pick from parfaits, hot fudge cream puffs, and homemade pie if you have room for dessert. Breakfast is served to overnight guests.

Seven spacious sleeping rooms occupy the second and third floors. They are very lovely and offer guests plenty of room to settle in comfortably for a few days to explore this old harbor city and the tip of Michigan's thumb.

Vitals

rooms: 7 that share 3 baths

children: no

pets: no

smoking: yes

open season: May through Labor Day, weekends Labor Day to January 1

rates: $65 through $75

rates include: breakfast and a bottle of champagne

owner/innkeeper:
Gary Regnier
8544 Lake Street
Port Austin, MI 48467
(517) 738-5254

Governor's Inn
Lexington

This handsome residence was built as a private home in 1859 by Charles Moore. At that time, Lexington was a major Great Lakes port. The trains carrying Michigan lumber bound for shipping ended at Lexington's docks, so pine was readily available and used extensively for the home's construction. The builder added a touch of elegance in the carved stairway and oak carpenter's lace, but otherwise the interior would have been considered quite simple in its day. The exterior is a different story, however, demonstrating several architectural styles including Italianate, Greek Revival, and Carpenter's Gothic.

On July 30, 1901, Charles Moore's youngest daughter, Mary, was married at the home to aspiring politician Albert (Bert) E. Sleeper, who became Michigan's governor in 1917. The Sleepers spent several summers there, where porch sitting and the simple life of a small town provided a retreat from the political spotlight.

Many decades later, the residence—now a bed-and-breakfast home—is still very much a "summer place." Jane and Bob MacDonald have furnished the inn and its three sleeping rooms with cotton rugs and Haywood-Wakefield wicker, iron beds, and light colored linens. Lace and eyelet curtains span many of the nearly floor-to-ceiling windows, yielding gracefully to the breezes off Lake Huron. The lines are clean, fresh, and uncluttered.

Continental breakfast is served in the first floor dining room at a great old table large enough to seat all the guests. But for those who wish, the fresh fruit and sweet cakes may also be eaten outside on the wraparound porch.

Lexington seems yet undiscovered by summer travelers. And that is

only one of the reasons to come visit this quiet harbor town. Boaters and anglers will find clean waters, great fishing, and a state-maintained marina. Lake Huron sailing is superb.

Jane and Bob know that many of their guests come to Lexington to get away from everything else. They have private living quarters in the inn and have developed a sixth sense for knowing when visitors want to chat and when they want to be alone. You will find them to be gracious hosts.

Vitals

rooms: 3 sleeping rooms, each with private bath

children: under 12 discouraged

pets: no

smoking: first floor only

open season: Memorial Day through mid-October

rates: $35 for two persons

rates include: Continental breakfast

owners/innkeepers:
    Jane and Bob MacDonald
    P.O. Box 471
    Lexington, MI 48450
    (313) 359-5770

The Homestead
Saline

If you remember the spring of 1986, you may remember the end of May, when it rained for seven days straight. We arrived at the Homestead on the eighth day under clear skies and found the season in full bloom. Cedar waxwings, barn swallows, and eastern orioles were in abundance. Trumpet vine and peony bushes were going through their decades-old ritual of sprouting fat buds. Trilliums and other wildflowers planted by Shirley Grossman, owner and innkeeper of the Homestead, were already bending under the weight of their blooms.

Shirley has occupied this farm estate since 1963, and although the home was built in 1851, her family was only the third to own it. They purchased it, furnished, from the Smith family, and among the treasures they received was a steamer chest full of arrowheads picked up in the surrounding fields by the elder Mr. Smith. This valley is rich in Indian history. The Saline River flows through the back of Shirley's property; it

was on its banks that the Indians used to set up camp to salt and preserve their fish, making use of the natural salt wells found throughout the area. It is from the wells that the river and city take their name. Michigan Avenue, just a mile north, was the east-west trail running between Detroit and Chicago.

Shirley raised five children in this home, and in 1984 she opened for bed-and-breakfast guests. Her six sleeping rooms are furnished with antiques and family heirlooms, including canopy and walnut bedsteads. Many of the furnishings belonged to the original owners. There is a comfortable mix here of turn-of-the-century elegance and the relaxed informality of a home that has been lived in and enjoyed for many decades and by many generations.

Shirley brings out crackers and cheese for guests in the early evening, which gives everyone a good opportunity to meet and mingle in the living room and parlor. She also keeps a steady supply of books, magazines, and daily newspapers on hand for her guests. Those who can play a tune are welcome to try their hand at the upright piano. The home has central heat, but wood-burning stoves in the parlor and dining room add to the coziness on cold days.

A full breakfast is served, with the offerings varying each day. We enjoyed dilled eggs and hot popovers with a selection of jellies and jams. The table was dressed with a soft pink lace cloth, fresh flowers, and candles. And each place was set with individual salt and pepper cellars. It was delightful.

If you are looking for shopping, music, theater, and dining, you can be in Ann Arbor or Ypsilanti in about fifteen minutes, and the town of Saline is just a half mile north.

Vitals

rooms: 6 that share 2 full baths

children: over 12 years of age

pets: no

smoking: yes

open season: year-round

rates: $25 through $50

rates include: breakfast

owner/innkeeper:
    Shirley Grossman
    9279 Macon Road
    Saline, MI 48176
    (313) 429-9625

Lake Street Manor
Port Austin

Looking at Lake Street Manor now, it is difficult to believe that at one time this lovely brick Victorian home was the local haunted house. According to owner Carolyn Greenwood, the windows were broken, it was covered over with vines, and it had suffered greatly from neglect.

Today, you will find this 1884 structure alive with activity. Carolyn purchased it in the spring of 1986 and opened it for bed-and-breakfast lodging and a whole lot more. First, there are four attractive sleeping rooms furnished with antiques. Guests are treated to a Continental breakfast in the morning and also have use of a large hot tub in front of the fireplace in the Bay Room. Color TV and in-room movies are available, as is room service from the nearby Bank 1884 restaurant.

Next, there is the antique shop located in the carriage house along with the Sarsaparilla Cafe, where sodas and snacks may be purchased by guests and the public for picnicking on the half-acre fenced grounds and gardens around the Manor. A gazebo and a pavilion with a small putting green complement the turn-of-the-century look. The P.A. Bike Rental, also on the premises, leases bikes by the hour or day, and the Great Lake Antique Photo Emporium in the inn parlor will document your fun with character photos while you wait. Lake Street Manor is located right on Port Austin's main street and is close to everything. This area has lots of summer recreational opportunities, including fishing and swimming, but Carolyn says the area also has a special beauty and peacefulness in the winter. Ask about winter getaway weekend packages.

Vitals

rooms: 4, 2 with private baths
children: over 12 years of age
pets: no
smoking: not in sleeping rooms, smoking rooms are available
open season: May through September, winter weekends
rates: $60 to $65 double occupancy
rates include: Continental breakfast
owner/innkeeper:
Carolyn Greenwood
8569 Lake Street (M-53)
Port Austin, MI 48467
(517) 738-7720

Mayflower Hotel
Plymouth

Ralph Lorenz began working at the Mayflower Hotel in 1939, and that is
where you will still find him today. The hotel was built in 1927 as the
joint venture of Plymouth's Rotary and Kiwanis clubs and the Chamber
of Commerce. It was their hope that the Mayflower would serve as a
focal point for town activities, and with Ralph's guidance for more than
forty-five years, it has. In 1964, he and his wife, Mabel, seized an opportunity to purchase the hotel. In 1981, Ralph received the Small Business
Association's National Senior Advocate of the Year Award for his leader-
ship and contributions in the city of Plymouth. It was bestowed by Vice-
President George Bush in the Rose Garden of the White House.

Located in the heart of this progressive community, the Mayflower has for decades been a source of innovative ideas. Years ago, it led the way in hospitality trends such as in-room air-conditioning and TVs. In the early 1970s, Ralph was inspired by a trip overseas to institute a bed-and-breakfast plan, and his tongue-in-cheek reason still makes guests chuckle . . . "More people eat than swim, so we included breakfast with the room instead of putting in a pool."

The hotel is flavored Early American and Colonial, with a nautical motif carried through in the pub and dining rooms. There is a feeling of warm elegance throughout the hotel along with an unprecedented friendliness offered by the employees, many of whom have worked at the hotel for several years, and by family members who have been raised up in the business. The sleeping rooms are large and tastefully decorated. They have all the standard first-class features such as direct-dial telephones, color TV, and private bathrooms. Those in the Mayflower II, a thirty-nine-room motor-hotel-style addition, also have refrigerators. Deluxe rooms and suites come with whirlpools and king-sized beds.

The food is as good as the hotel boasts. Among their innovative offerings are fine vintage European and American wines that can be served by the glass, thanks to the steward's use of Michigan's first nitrogen wine preservation system, called a Cruvinet. The complimentary breakfast is a full meal—guests have their choice of eggs, pancakes, bacon or sausages, cereals, and beverages.

In 1983, son Scott, who is now the hotel's general manager, implemented the brilliant idea of a par value program in the hotel, giving visiting Canadians face value for their Canadian dollars. The hotel is ideally suited to tour groups and the staff makes them feel welcome immediately on arrival by rolling out an actual red carpet.

Across from the hotel is the town square, site of dances, art fairs, band concerts, and the Mayflower's nationally known ice sculpture spectacular. If you want to plan your visit to coincide with a truly breathtaking event, ask about the Mayflower's annual hot-air balloon festival held each July. Within minutes of the hotel, you can watch the horses race at Northville Downs and select from seven golf courses. Less than half an hour away are Ann Arbor, Metro Airport, Greenfield Village, Tiger Stadium, and the Renaissance Center.

Vitals

rooms: 100 with private baths; some also have a private whirlpool

children: yes

pets: no

smoking: yes

open season: year-round

rates: $45 through $75 single, $55 through $85 double

rates include: full breakfast

owner: Ralph Lorenz

innkeepers:

    Scott Lorenz
    Randy Lorenz
    Creon Smith
    827 West Ann Arbor Trail
    Plymouth, MI 48170
    (313) 453-1620

Montague Inn
Saginaw

This magnificent Georgian-style mansion was built for the Montague family between 1928 and 1929. Among its numerous outstanding original features are half-a-dozen Art Deco tiled baths, built-in library bookshelves with secret passages, pegged oak floors, and deep bay windows. But perhaps the most incredible aspect of this home is that it was built for a family of four. Its full size is not apparent from the street because a long wing that extends from the back of the home is not visible from the front. That was a trend in design during the Depression, presumably because the owners did not wish to flaunt their wealth. If you step out to the back gardens, take a brief stroll toward Lake Linton, and turn to face the home again, you will be better able to appreciate the dimensions of this majestic estate. It sits on eight and one-half parklike acres, and Lake Linton is its western border.

Owners Les and Marian Tincknell, Norm and Kathryn Kinney, and Aaron and Ann Acker purchased the home in July, 1985, and after several months of restoration work, opened it as an inn in May, 1986. It is elegant and exceptionally comfortable, with fine furnishings befitting the period including many large Oriental and Persian rugs. Thirteen sleeping rooms occupy the mansion and another five are located in the adjacent guesthouse.

A first-floor dining room in the mansion serves lunch and dinner Tuesday through Saturday by reservation only. Prices range from five to ten dollars for lunch entrées and fifteen to twenty-four dollars for dinner. A Continental breakfast is served to overnight guests.

The number of common rooms and the availability of full food service make Montague Inn well suited for small business meetings and conferences, receptions, and parties. The inn had been open barely three months when we met the Tincknells and innkeeper Carole Kiefer there in August, but it appeared from our brief visit to be an immediate and well-deserved success.

Vitals

rooms: 18, 16 with private baths

children: yes

pets: no

smoking: common areas only

open season: year-round

rates: $40 through $90 single, add $5 per room double occupancy

rates include: Continental breakfast

owners: Les and Marian Tincknell, Norm and Kathryn Kinney, Aaron and Ann Acker

innkeeper:
Carole Kiefer
1581 South Washington
Saginaw, MI 48601
(517) 752-3939

Murphy Inn
St. Clair

The Murphy Inn has been hosting overnight guests since 1836, and according to owner Ron Sabotka, it is the oldest commercial building in St. Clair. In fact, it occupied the site before the city of St. Clair was platted. When Ron and his wife, Nancy, bought it in June, 1985, they decided to retain its original name. A lot of people had been staying there for years, explained Ron, "And no matter what we might call it, it would always be known as the Murphy Inn!"

This place is a lot of fun. The main floor has a casual, country-theme

dining room on one side and a bar on the other, with a combined capacity of eighty people. The back bar was built in 1906 by the Brunswick Company and is set off handsomely by the room's kelly green and white print wallpaper. Much of the clientele is local, which is usually a sign of good food and personable service. We found both to be true. The staff was friendly and chatty, and the nachos and sandwiches were great, as promised. Also included on the menu were turkey and roast beef croissants, diet plates, salads, and cheesecakes. Our only regret was that we could not stay through Saturday night, when they pack the place for a singalong.

During renovation of the inn, the original twelve small upstairs sleeping rooms were combined to make seven large rooms with private baths. They have been extensively redecorated with beautiful print wallpapers and plush carpeting. The beds are all new and very comfortable. Nearly all the wooden turn-of-the-century dressers, vanities, and washstands have been in the hotel for several decades. Extra insulation went into the floors to improve soundproofing. Later in the evening, we could occasionally hear quiet laughter drifting up from the bar. It is a pleasant sound, that of friends having a good time, and we drifted effortlessly off to sleep.

Many of the inn's overnight guests come to St. Clair by boat and dock at the marina just half a block away. Guests who golf can enjoy playing at the St. Clair Golf Club, where special arrangements can be made for them through the inn. Two other courses are within fifteen miles. Those who want to take a stroll may head for the boardwalk. It is said to be the longest ever built along fresh water.

Vitals

rooms: 7 with private baths

children: yes

pets: no

smoking: yes

open season: year-round

rates: $52 through $75 double occupancy

rates include: Continental breakfast

owners/innkeepers:

    Ron and Nancy Sabotka
    505 Clinton
    St. Clair, MI 48079
    (313) 329-7118

Oakbrook Inn
Davison

This magnificent pillared mansion is located back from the road in a parklike setting of rolling lawn and mature trees. Oakbrook's original two-story section and west wing were built in 1938. The east wing, with its large lounge area, was added thirty years later, and it is there that guests are most often greeted by owners Jan and Bill Cooke. They are easygoing, amiable hosts who have brought to this majestic structure the classic warmth and pace of a casual country inn.

Their lounge is furnished at one end with big, comfortable groupings of couches and chairs, a TV, and a pool table. At the other end are tables where breakfast is served and guests gather to chat over cups of coffee. Beyond the lounge is an enclosed twenty-by-forty-foot pool and an adjacent built-in bar with a refrigerator where guests may store beverages.

There are seven sleeping rooms, all spacious and very pretty. Print

wallpapers set off lovely antique bedsteads and an assortment of oak washstands, vanities, dressers, and handsome glass lamps. You will also find hand-stitched quilts and pillows that were made by Jan. The three second-floor rooms are reached by a sweeping stairway that wraps around the original main entrance. Another three are just off the pool area, including the huge Master Bedroom that has a sauna and a sunken tub with a whirlpool. The entire home is plushly carpeted, tastefully decorated, and comfortable.

Jan and Bill opened Oakbrook for bed-and-breakfast lodging in spring, 1985. They are gracious innkeepers, and they spend as much time with their guests as possible. The home seems especially well suited for small groups and conferences. Often, says Jan, it is rented by friends who just want to get away for a few days and relax. A Continental breakfast is served each morning. Catered meals for groups can be arranged. For extended stays, you may want to inquire about the small two-bedroom cottage on the property. It is available for minimum stays of one week and has complete cooking facilities.

Vitals

rooms: 7 in the inn, 5 with private full baths, 2 have private half baths
  and share a shower

children: over 10 years of age

pets: no

smoking: lounge area only

open season: year-round

rates: $45 through $80 double occupancy

rates include: Continental breakfast

owners/innkeepers:
  Jan and Bill Cooke
  7256 East Court Street
  Davison, MI 48423
  (313) 658-1546
  (313) 653-1744

Raymond House Inn
Port Sanilac

Oliver Raymond was in his mid-eighties when Shirley Denison purchased his family's home from him, and he is the third generation of Raymonds to have lived there. Oliver still lives just down the street. He is a frequent visitor at the inn and provides Shirley and her guests with firsthand history of the estate. We had the privilege of meeting Mr. Raymond one evening when he came to visit. We learned that the bedroom adjacent to the dining room was for years the birthing room, and it was there, around the turn of the century, that he and several siblings were born.

Grandfather Uri Raymond came to Port Sanilac in 1850 and established a successful mercantile business. He built the handsome brick home with its distinctive white icicle trim in 1871. Shirley attributes the excellent condition of the house to the fact that it was in the same family for more than one hundred years and was never left empty or abandoned.

Shirley spent her childhood summers in Port Sanilac and had long admired the stately Raymond home. When it came up for sale, she knew she had to have it. She also knew that she would make very few changes, wanting it to closely resemble the days when three generations of Raymonds walked its wide and tall-ceilinged halls.

There are six sleeping rooms open to guests, and they are all large, bright, and colorfully decorated. Like the parlor and dining room, they are furnished with lovely antiques, rockers, handloomed rugs, and lacy curtains as well as many old photographs. Some of the rooms have sitting areas, and there are dressers so guests can unpack for a few days. This is a good place to come with a stack of books, a list of unwritten letters, or a folio of unfinished reports. During July and August, Shirley's

husband, Ray, will take guests for day sails, and if you are interested in antique shopping, you will not even have to leave the inn. Shirley's sister, Barbara Gruenwald, has opened a cozy shop on the third floor. A Continental breakfast is served each morning in the formal dining room or on an adjacent patio.

While innkeeping in this picturesque harbor town may be a relatively new career to Shirley, surrounding herself with history and art is not. For several years, she worked as a restorative artist for museums and in the United States Capitol, and she has exhibited her own sculpture and pottery in galleries in the East. Shirley's gallery and studio at the Raymond House Inn feature her wheel-thrown pottery, which is glazed and fired on the premises.

Vitals

rooms: 6 rooms with private baths

children: discouraged

pets: no

smoking: parlor only

open season: May through October

rates: $45 double occupancy Sunday through Friday, $50 Saturday

rates include: Continental breakfast

owner/innkeeper:

    Shirley Denison

    111 S. Ridge Street (M-25)

    Port Sanilac, MI 48469

    (313) 622-8800

Vickie Van's Bed and Breakfast
Lexington

Vickie Van's bed-and-breakfast home is filled with personal treasures, and around most of the pieces is woven a story. "These are all the things I've grown up with," she said as she gestured around the room. She pointed to a mannequin in the corner wearing a pale pink, lace-trimmed dress, the same dress her mother is wearing in a nearby portrait painted several years ago. There are other family pictures and furnishings that have been passed on to Vickie from her parents. They are fine pieces, like the canopy and brass beds that are accented with beautiful linens and the turn-of-the-century wicker. Lace curtains in all the windows add a romantic touch.

Vickie bought the home in February, 1985, and opened the following June. One of her unexpected pleasures was getting the chance to talk with a woman who had lived in the home nearly fifty years ago. Tax records indicate that the structure was built in 1847. It sits on five acres,

and if you hit the season right, you can help Vickie pick blackberries from her bushes. When we talked to her in mid-August they were heavy with fruit. Vickie can also direct you to several pick-your-own fruit farms in the area for blueberries, raspberries, and strawberries.

Guests often gather in the game and TV room. It is informal and cozy—just a few steps down from the adjacent kitchen where Vickie is often busy preparing treats for the next morning. Breakfast varies daily, with selections that include homemade muffins, croissants, cheese and sausage, juices, and fresh fruit or fruit salad. It is served on dishes that belonged to Vickie's grandmother.

"All my dreams are coming true here," Vickie said unabashedly. She thoroughly enjoys running a bed-and-breakfast home and cares deeply

for her guests. "Every person is a story," she recounted. "People open up to me and they talk a lot here. I try to make each person's day a little bit better."

Vitals

rooms: 4, 2 with private baths and 2 that share 1 bath

children: limited accommodations

pets: no

smoking: in the game and TV room only

open season: year-round

rates: $38 single, $43 double

rates include: breakfast

owner/innkeeper:

Vickie Van
5076 South Lakeshore Road
Lexington, MI 48450
(313) 359-5533

The Victorian Inn
Port Huron

This fine Queen Anne structure was designed by architect Isaac Erb and built as a residence for James A. Davidson and his family in 1896. Davidson grew up in Port Huron and established a huge home furnishings company there that occupied three adjacent storefronts on Military Street.

Ed and Vicki Peterson and Lew and Lynne Secory became the home's fourth set of owners when they purchased it in 1983. They were pleased to find that the original plans and specification sheets passed on to them were still in good order, providing great assistance in the renovation. Three months after their purchase, the home was judged historically and architecturally significant by the Michigan Historical Commission and was listed on the State Register of Historic Places.

The four second-floor sleeping rooms are furnished with period pieces, particularly Queen Anne, and dressed with yards of lace and

finery. Warm tones of peach and rose are used for most of the walls, linens, and floor coverings. They provide a backdrop for Victorian-era memorabilia such as a collection of hatboxes, a nosegay, a wicker bed tray, and a beribboned wreath of baby's breath and dried flowers. The effect is romantic and very pretty.

The inn's elegant first-floor dining room is open to the public, with lunch and dinner offerings such as beef rosettes with duxelles, veal chops with morel sauce, the chef's special cream of peanut soup, and homemade ice cream. The floor staff is formally attired—a very appropriate touch in such a genteel setting. The cellar has been converted to Pierpont's Pub, where stone walls and an embossed tin ceiling lend a more casual atmosphere. It features live music on Thursday and Friday nights.

A Continental breakfast of freshly baked croissants, coffee, and juice is served each morning to overnight guests.

Vitals

rooms: 4, 2 with private baths

children: yes

pets: no

smoking: yes

open season: year-round

rates: $45 through $60 per double room

rates include: Continental breakfast

owners/innkeepers:
>Ed and Vicki Peterson
>Lew and Lynne Secory
>1229 7th Street
>Port Huron, MI 48060
>(313) 984-1437

Bed-and-Breakfast Reservation Services

The following descriptions are of bed-and-breakfast reservation services. Although we have not used any of the services and have not visited all the homes they represent, we offer them to you as another means of locating bed-and-breakfast lodging at your destination point.

Bed and Breakfast of Grand Rapids
Grand Rapids

The Heritage Hill district of Grand Rapids boasts representation of more than sixty architectural styles—the largest collection of any historic district in the country. The homes were built between 1850 and 1920, and they cover several blocks on the eastern perimeter of the downtown.

Bed and Breakfast of Grand Rapids is a reservation service that places overnight guests in private homes within the historic district. A variety of accommodations are available. Coordinator Joyce Makinen provides a reservation request form to help match the special needs and interests of guests with the offerings of host families. She also coordinates historic home tours of the area.

This is an excellent opportunity to learn about the district and to spend some time in marvelous historic homes that you might otherwise only see from the sidewalk.

Bed and Breakfast of Grand Rapids
344 College S.E.
Grand Rapids, MI 49503
(616) 451-4849 or (616) 456-7121

Betsy Ross Bed and Breakfast in Michigan

Diane Shields is the new owner of this reservation service and has listings throughout the Lower Peninsula of Michigan. Most accommodations are in private homes or small guesthouses located in the Detroit area as well as Ann Arbor, the thumb region, and northern resort areas. To secure reservations, send Diane a self-addressed stamped envelope and request a directory of her participating homes. She updates it frequently. Each listing includes a brief description of the home or guesthouse and its general location. You can also call Diane after 6:00 P.M. and on weekends. Room rates range from thirty-five through fifty-five dollars double occupancy, with a single about ten dollars less.

Betsy Ross Bed and Breakfast in Michigan
Diane Shields
P.O. Box 1731
Dearborn, MI 48121-1731
(313) 561-6041

Dutch Country Bed and Breakfast Reservation Service
Holland

Dutch Country Reservation Service offers bed-and-breakfast lodging in several private homes in the Holland and Zeeland area. Both city and rural homes, including working farms, are available. Some will accommodate children or pets, as well as those who speak a foreign language or are handicapped. A Continental breakfast with fruit or juice, baked goods, coffee, and tea is served to all overnight guests.

Dutch Country Bed and Breakfast Reservation Service
6491 Spruce Lane
Holland, MI 49423
(616) 396-3344

Frankenmuth Area Bed and Breakfast Reservation Service
Frankenmuth

If you plan to partake in the Bavarian-style festivities of the town of Frankenmuth, you can reserve bed-and-breakfast accommodations through this local reservation service. Host homes offer from two to four sleeping rooms. Reservations are made through a central number and payment is made directly to the reservation service rather than the host. Coordinator Beverley Bender says that promotes the feeling of being a guest in the home. Early reservations are helpful, but drop-ins are welcome. Rates range from forty through sixty dollars double occupancy with a Continental breakfast.

> Frankenmuth Area Bed and Breakfast Reservation Service
> 337 Trinklein Street
> Frankenmuth, MI 48734
> Beverley Bender
> (517) 652-8897
> Doris Schmitzer
> (517) 652-6747

Index

Adrian
  Rosewood Country Inn, 175
Allegan
  The Winchester Inn, 133
Alpena
  Fireside Inn, 50
Apple Beach Inn, Northport, 33

Bay Bed and Breakfast, Charlevoix,
  36
Bed and Breakfast of Grand Rapids,
  Grand Rapids, 224
Bed and Breakfast of Ludington,
  Ludington, 38
Bed and Breakfast Reservation
  Services
  Bed and Breakfast of Grand
    Rapids, Grand Rapids, 224
  Betsy Ross Bed and Breakfast in
    Michigan, 225
  Dutch Country Bed and Breakfast
    Reservation Service, Holland,
    226
  Frankenmuth Area Bed and Break-
    fast Reservation Service, Fran-
    kenmuth, 227
Betsy Ross Bed and Breakfast in
  Michigan, 225
Beulah
  Brookside Inn, 40
  Windermere Inn, 85
Blue Lake Lodge, Mecosta, 141
Bogan Lane Inn, Mackinac Island, 11
The Botsford Inn, Farmington Hills,
  189
Brookside Inn, Beulah, 40

Chaffin Farms Bed and Breakfast,
  Ithaca, 144
Charlevoix
  Bay Bed and Breakfast, 36
  The Patchwork Parlour
    Bed'n'Breakfast, 71

Chimney Corners, Frankfort, 43
Clifford Lake Hotel, Stanton, 146
Colonial House Inn and Motel, St.
  Ignace, 14
Country Cottage, Maple City, 46

Davison
  Oakbrook Inn, 210
Douglas
  Rosemont Inn, 122
Dutch Country Bed and Breakfast
  Reservation Service, Holland, 226

E. E. Douville Bed and Breakfast,
  Manistee, 47
Ellsworth
  The House on the Hill, 58
Escanaba
  House of Ludington, 23

Farmington Hills
  The Botsford Inn, 189
Fennville
  Hidden Pond Farm, 96
Fireside Inn, Alpena, 50
Frankenmuth
  Frankenmuth Area Bed and Break-
    fast Reservation Service, 227
Frankenmuth Area Bed and Break-
  fast Reservation Service, Fran-
  kenmuth, 227
Frankfort
  Chimney Corners, 43

The Garfield Inn, Port Austin, 192
Gordon Beach Inn, Union Pier, 93
Governor's Inn, Lexington, 195
Grand Rapids
  Bed and Breakfast of Grand
    Rapids, 224
Grist Mill Guest House, Homer,
  149
Gulls' Way, Petoskey, 54

Haan Cottage, Mackinac Island, 17
Hall House Bed and Breakfast, Kalamazoo, 152
Hansen's Guest House, Homer, 155
Harbor Springs
    Harbour Inn on the Bay, 55
Harbour Inn on the Bay, Harbor Springs, 55
Helmer House Inn, McMillan, 20
Hidden Pond Farm, Fennville, 96
Holland
    Dutch Country Bed and Breakfast Reservation Service, 226
    The Parsonage 1915, 115
Homer
    Grist Mill Guest House, 149
    Hansen's Guest House, 155
The Homestead, Saline, 198
House of Ludington, Escanaba, 23
The House on the Hill, Ellsworth, 58

The Inn at Union Pier, Union Pier, 98
Ithaca
    Chaffin Farms Bed and Breakfast, 144

Jonesville
    Munro House Bed and Breakfast, 164

Kalamazoo
    Hall House Bed and Breakfast, 152
    Stuart Avenue Inn, 181
Kemah Guest House, Saugatuck, 101
The Kirby House, Saugatuck, 104

Lakeside
    Pebble House, 116
Lake Street Manor, Port Austin, 201
Lamont
    The Stagecoach Stop, 128
The Last Resort, South Haven, 107
Leelanau Country Inn, Maple City, 61
Leeland
    The Riverside Inn, 75
Lexington
    Governor's Inn, 195

Vickie Van's Bed and Breakfast, 216
Ludington
    Bed and Breakfast of Ludington, 38

McCarthy's Bear Creek Inn, Marshall, 156
Mackinac Island
    Bogan Lane Inn, 11
    Haan Cottage, 17
    Stonecliffe, 27
McMillan
    Helmer House Inn, 20
Manistee
    E. E. Douville Bed and Breakfast, 47
Manistique
    Marina Guest House, 26
Maple City
    Country Cottage, 46
    Leelanau Country Inn, 61
Marina Guest House, Manistique, 26
Marshall
    McCarthy's Bear Creek Inn, 156
    National House Inn, 167
Mayflower Hotel, Plymouth, 202
Mecosta
    Blue Lake Lodge, 141
Mendon
    The Mendon Country Inn, 159
The Mendon Country Inn, Mendon, 159
Montague
    Morning Glory Inn, 110
Montague Inn, Saginaw, 205
Morning Glory Inn, Montague, 110
Mulberry House, Owosso, 162
Munro House Bed and Breakfast, Jonesville, 164
Murphy Inn, St. Clair, 207

National House Inn, Marshall, 167
Neahtawanta Inn, Traverse City (Bowers Harbor), 64
Niles
    Yesterday's Inn Bed and Breakfast, 136